GW01018092

Geckoes

Uroplatus guentheri, of which several pair may be kept together.

Geckoes

Biology, Husbandry, and Reproduction

Friedrich-Wilhelm Henkel
Wolfgang Schmidt

Translated from the
original German by
JOHN HACKWORTH

KRIEGER PUBLISHING COMPANY
MALABAR, FLORIDA
1995

Original German Edition 1991
1st English Edition 1995

Printed and Published by
KRIEGER PUBLISHING COMPANY
KRIEGER DRIVE
MALABAR, FLORIDA 32950

Library of Congress Cataloging-In-Publication Data

Henkel, Friedrich-Wilhelm.
   [Geckoes English]
   Geckoes : biology, husbandry, and reproduction / Friedrich-Wilhelm Henkel, Wolfgang Schmidt ; translated from the original German by John Hackworth.
   p. cm.
   Includes bibliographical references (p.) and index.
   1. Captive geckos. I. Schmidt, Wolfgang. II. Title.
SF515.5.G43H4613   1995
ISBN 0-89464-919-1
639.3'95—dc20   94-36667
                                             CIP

10 9 8 7 6 5 4 3 2

Front Cover Photo:
Oedura castelnaui (Fat-Tailed Gecko).

Contents

Contents

Acknowledgements

We would like to express our grateful thanks to Dr. Wolfgang Böhme of Bonn for numerous invaluable comments and suggestions and for providing much obscure literature as well as for the critical examination of the manuscript.

In addition we would like to thank all gecko-keepers who have given us assistance enabling us to obtain further information, especially Horst and Markus Juschka, Düsseldorf; Klaus Liebel, Herne; Joachim Sameit, Bergkamen; Erich Schröder, Kiel; Robert Seip, Frankfurt; Harald Simon, Dreieich; Thomas Ulber, Berlin; and Roland Zobel, Herne.

Bergkamen and Soest
February, 1991.

Friedrich-Wilhelm Henkel
Wolfgang Schmidt

Foreword

Over 100 years ago in his *Catalogue of Lizards in the British Museum of Natural History* (1885) George A. Boulenger compiled all information available to him at the time and was able to distinguish 53 genera with a total of 313 species; at that time subspecies were not known. Eighty years later (1965) *Das Tierreich* appeared and this is now considered to be a more valid and concise list of existing geckoes. As a result of the newly discovered and described forms, the number had increased to 73 genera, 668 species and 257 subspecies. To compile the list in *Das Tierreich* was an enormous undertaking, but I was compelled to do it since none of my colleagues expressed a readiness to do so. However, the outcome was recognised. At the time it had also become the fashion amongst certain "colleagues" to pick holes in a large publication by another author if it did not correspond exactly to one's own ideas and opinions.

I suspect that in the meantime the number of distinguishable geckoes has increased by around ten percent, whereby these animals are by far the largest and most divergent group of all present-day lizards. Despite the increasing difficulty of surveying this multiplicity of species, there was also the problem of dealing with the largest possible number of gecko species. This presented a certain risk for the meritorious authors but I do not think they may expect any criticism from experts. They have managed to condense an enormous amount of data from scientific and herpetological publications and have presented this book as a harmonious entity.

The authors decided, quite rightly, that it was not their task to deal individually with each of the known species and subspecies and thankfully they have also not touched upon the abstract questions of sys-

xi

tematics and nomenclature because these problems can change almost daily. In this respect, herpetologists should be directed towards the greatest possible stability. The authors have approached these matters by presenting the various points of view in the most clear and concise way. They have done this by grouping together species which are related or have similar lifestyles, without becoming bogged-down in the minutae which in this book would only be surplus ballast.

Anyone who is familiar with the subject and the difficulties attached to universal synopses will immediately realise that here we have competent and very successful keepers and breeders of geckoes who present their vast experience to other herpetologists in a very able, concise, and well-thought-out way. Although the authors have not considered one species or another, this should not detract from the enormous value of the work. Should anyone nevertheless choose to complain, let him by all means do so. . . . .and then present us with an improved version.

Dr. Heinz Wermuth.

Friedrich-Wilhelm Henkel and *Wolfgang Schmidt* are the foremost keepers and breeders of geckoes in Germany, and they have over 20 years' experience. They have traveled extensively collecting these fascinating animals and have written countless articles on all aspects of gecko husbandry for numerous publications both at home and overseas. Their works continue to be translated into several languages.

John Hackworth, a recognized translator, is also an amateur herpetologist and keeps a variety of snakes, geckoes, and other lizards.

Rain forest in New Caledonia.

Lifestyle, Appearance, and Distribution of Geckoes

Amongst the vertebrates, the family Gekkonidae belongs to the class of reptiles and the squamata group of lizards. This is an enormously diverse and ancient family of lizards which has a very long history.

EVOLUTIONARY HISTORY

The squamata originated around 195 million years ago during the Triassic period. It was only much later however, around 50 million years ago, that the present family of Gekkonidae evolved, presumably from the Jurassic families of Ardeosauridae and Bavarisauridae. However, because of a shortage of fossilised animals their exact evolutionary history is not known. The oldest finds of true geckoes originate from the Eoscene period when they adapted to the most divergent conditions and habitats.

Nowadays, the region of origin of the family Gekkonidae is accepted as being Southeast Asia because, there, the original forms, geckoes of the genus *Aeluroscalabotes*, can still be found. Because of their enormous capacity for adaptation, geckoes have become extremely cosmopolitan since the Eoscene period and have adapted to the most divergent conditions and most widely varying habitats.

SYSTEMATICS

Since the Wermuth list of 1965, no one has undertaken the formidable task of a total revision of the Gekkonidae family. At that time Wermuth divided the family into 4 subfamilies with 670 species.

Today it is very difficult to reach agreement on the systematics since species, genera, and even subfamilies are frequently newly designated. A survey of the current position gives the following picture. In addition, each year numerous new species are discovered, thus rounding off an extending picture of the entire family.

DISTRIBUTION AND HABITAT

Since around the Eoscene period geckoes have colonised almost the whole world. It can be roughly stated that they live on all continents and almost all islands between latitudes 50° N. and 50° S. (see distribution map on page 4).

We have attempted to divide the map of the world into distinct colonisation regions in which certain species, genera, and subfamilies occur so that it can be easily seen to which distribution range a given gecko species may be assigned.

Around 1000 years ago the actual distribution of some species corresponded to this map, but since the beginning of long sea voyages numerous species have become distributed worldwide. Many of these "stowaways" died immediately because they could not compete with the endemic creatures. However, because of their extreme adaptability, some species were able to find new habitats and colonised every available niche. Thus, for example, *Hemidactylus frenatus* can now be found in almost any port in which the climate allows it to survive.

Because of their excellent adaptability geckoes have colonised a wide variety of biotopes and their habitats include the most divergent ecological niches. Some species inhabit the shoreline of the sea, others live on sandy beaches, cliff faces, forests, and even high mountains. Numerous species of geckoes may even be found in the most inhospitable deserts on earth. These species have evolved to become active at night rather than during the day, thus avoiding the extremely high temperatures.

To keep geckoes properly it is essential to know the origins of the animals. It is also essential to know how the animals live in their natural habitat. Do they live on or below tree bark, in holes in trees, in

Class: Reptiles (Reptilia)
Order: True reptiles (Squamata)
Suborder: Lizards (Sauria)
Intermediate order: Gecko-like (Gekkota)

Family: Geckoes (Gekkonidae) Fin-feet (Pygopodidae)*
Subfamily

Lidded Geckoes**	Double-fingered Geckoes	True Geckoes	Ball-fingered Geckoes
Eublepharinae	Diplodactylinae	Gekkoninae	Sphaerodacty linae
6 genera	15 genera	64 genera	5 genera
ca. 20 species	ca. 100 species	ca. 600 species	ca. 100 species
Subspecies	Subspecies	Subspecies	Subspecies

*) In the opinion of Kluge (1987) the Fin-feet are more closely related to the Diplo-dactylinae than to other geckoes.

**)The Lidded Geckoes are now usually considered to be only one family, Euble-pharidae, (Grismer, 1988).

bushes, beneath rocks, in rock crevices, or amongst foliage? Do they dig their own burrows or take over those abandoned by other creatures? There are different answers to these questions for each species, and these are considered in the species descriptions which follow. It is of course much better if one has the opportunity to personally observe the animals in their natural habitat.

For example: The Helmeted Gecko, *Geckonia chazaliae*, inhabits the sand dunes directly on the coast of Morocco. It is usually found below dried-out camel dung and only rarely beneath rocks or driftwood. The reason for this is as follows: During the day the camel dung is heated uniformly, whilst underneath it always remains somewhat moist. These conditions attract a considerable number of woodlice and other insects upon which the gecko feeds. The small distribution range of this species is also allied to the high rainfall since the Canary Current runs along the coast of Morocco.

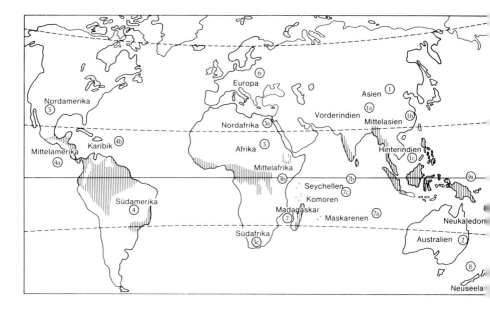

Distribution ranges of geckoes on the individual continents.

1 Asia; 1a Near India; 1b Central Asia; 1c Far East.
2 Australia.
3 Africa; 3a North Africa; 3b Central Africa; 3c South Africa.
4 South America; 4a Central America; 4b Caribbean.
5 North America.
6 Europe.
7 Madagascar; 7a Mascarenes; 7b Seychelles; 7c Comoros.
8 New Zealand.
9 New Caledonia; 9a Oceania.

This shows how different the habitats of the various gecko species can be and the factors which must be taken into consideration to be able to keep them properly in captivity. In the tables which precede the species descriptions an attempt has been made to allocate each of the genera to a typical biotope:
A = ground dwellers
B = tree dwellers
C = bush dwellers
D = cliff dwellers

Above: Nephrurus asper laying eggs.
Left: Habitat of several Rhacodactylus species.
Right: Habitat of Eurodactylodes and several Bavayia species.

Above: Habitat of several Australian terrestrial geckoes.
Below: Habitat of Phyllurus platurus.

BUILD AND MIMICRY

Amongst the reptiles, the geckoes are a very diverse group. This diversity is founded on their ability to adapt to the most divergent biotopes and climates, because in appearance the Gekkonidae family is a very homogeneous group. The body is usually cylindrical and squat whilst somewhat flattened on the upper side. In most cases the skin consists of fine scales and feels rather like velvet. Some species do however have scales which are overlapped like roof tiles. The limbs are usually well and uniformly developed. The head is large and mostly well set-off from the neck. The large prominent eyes are especially conspicuous.

These animals do however vary considerably in size. The largest of all known geckoes is *Hoplodactylus delcourti*, the only known specimen of which had a total length of over 60 cm. This giant gecko was not discovered in its native New Zealand, but by Bauer (1986) as a dry-preparation in the Natual History Museum of Marseille, where it had been placed during the last century.

Because in those days animals used to be considerably stretched whilst being dry-prepared, Bauer x-rayed the gecko and found that this was indeed the actual length of the animal. Unfortunately, no further animals of this species are known from New Zealand.

The largest geckoes living today are *Gekko gecko* with a total length of around 35 cm, and *Rhacodactylus leachianus, Uroplatus fimbriatus*, and *Gekko smithii*, each with a total length of over 35 cm. Because of its stout and robust build, *Rhacodactylus leachianus* is an especially imposing lizard.

The smallest living geckoes are from the subfamily Sphaerodactylinae, e.g., *Lepidoblepharis s. sanctaemartae* with a maximum total length of around 40 mm and *Sphaerodactylus nicholsi* with a total length of only around 28 mm.

As well as in size and colouring, there are also some variations in body shape which would not normally be attributed to geckoes. For example, some ground-dwelling geckoes of the genera *Nephrurus* and *Geckonia* have only a very short body, whilst superficially *Geckonia chazaliae* resembles an agama.

A further peculiarity in appearance is presented by the skin borders and folds of skin along the sides of the body of some gecko species. These occur in all variations. They range from only slightly formed skin folds in the case of *Lepidodactylus lugubris* to the large folds of skin along both sides of the body of geckoes of the genera *Uroplatus* and *Ptychozoon*. This protective adaptation is usually reinforced by special camouflage colouring so that it is almost impossible to see the animals when they are resting on tree bark. This mimicry is best illustrated by the genus *Uroplatus*. Not only does it imitate the bark, but its colouring also imitates fissures and lichens. The purpose of the skin folds is to prevent the animal's casting a shadow whilst lying at rest on a tree. To do this they open up the skin fold completely and thus blend in with the bark.

Such animals usually have only a very short fleeing distance, relying mainly on their camouflage for protection. If they are molested in any way they seek safety by fleeing and jumping to the next tree or simply by running away from their aggressor.

It has been proven that geckoes of the genus *Ptychozoon* can glide for short distances; the Flying Geckoes use their skin folds as a type of sail in a way similar to that of the Flying Lizards of the genus *Draco*. Geckoes of the genus *Uroplatus* also use their tails as a sort of rudder when gliding from tree to tree.

A further instance of mimicry has been observed amongst the small *Uroplatus* species. *Uroplatus ebenaui* hangs in bushes resembling vegetation and to date no one has ever found one of these geckoes in the wild during the day. Even in a vivarium they are often difficult to find.

SKIN AND SCALATION

The main function of the skin of a gecko is to protect it from all external influences. As well as mechanical protection, the skin is especially important as protection against water and heat loss. The skin guarantees these defences perfectly.

The construction of the skin in all reptiles is the same. It consists of three different layers. The multi-layered outer skin (epidermis) forms the actual protection against all external influences. As a result of constant cell division in the lowermost layer, new cells are regularly pushed upwards. These cells contain keratin which causes the build up

Eublepharis macularius sloughing. This species eats its skin.

of a horny layer which does not grow with the animal and which is frequently rubbed off against any available solid object. In this way the epidermis is renewed by regular sloughing. Young animals slough more frequently than adults because the epidermis does not grow with them. The first slough occurs shortly after hatching.

That sloughing is imminent is indicated by the skin becoming lighter, after which it begins to split, usually starting at the snout, and falls away in large pieces. The gecko will then attempt to remove the remaining pieces of skin. This they do actively, using the mouth and limbs. Some species always eat the old skin, whilst others never do so.

Left: Skin injury on Ailuronyx.
Right: Skin injury on Geckolepis.

Below the epidermis there is the leather skin (dermis), which consists of a connecting tissue with elastic membranes. In this can be found the blood vessels, nerves, sensory nerves, skin muscles, and colour cells. The third layer is the lower skin (subcutis). This connects the skin to the muscles lying below it.

The skin of geckoes does not have many glands. The only obvious glands are those on the tails of some *Diplodactylus* and *Eurodactylus* species. These emit a foul-smelling secretion which is sometimes sprayed at aggressors (Rosenberg & Russell, 1980). Externally the skin is seen as a coat of scales. This scalation, which is characteristic for the species and group, has a certain degree of variation within each species. Nevertheless, it is a very useful characteristic for determination and for the systematics. A basic distinction can be made between the two types of scalation (see page 11): Small adjacent scales (granula) with scattered tubercles; and large scales overlapped in the manner of roof tiles.

Most species have granular scalation which can be variable. The scales may be different in size and appearance and can have one or more keels. They may also have tubercles or spikes. Often the scalation on the head, the limbs, and the tail is different from that on the body. Thus there are large, plate-like scales on the head whilst the upper sides of the limbs, the back, and the tail may be covered by tubercular

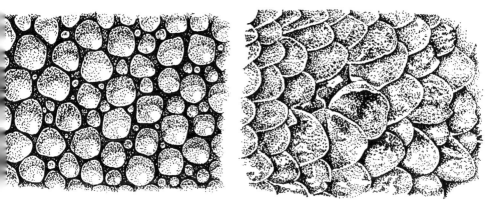

The two types of scalation. Granular scalation (left) and plate-like scales overlapping in the manner of roof tiles (right).

scales. The scales on the back and tail are usually arranged in parallel longitudinal rows. Especially noticeable are the spiny scales on the tail (in, for example, *Diplodactylus ciliaris*) or above the eyes or on the back as in *Uroplatus fantasticus*.

Only the two genera *Geckolepis* and *Teratoscincus* have totally different scalation. They have large plate-like scales which are overlapped in the manner of roof tiles, similar to the scales on fish. In this type of scalation the skin is not so strongly attached to the muscles lying beneath it, so that *Teratoscincus* are able to breathe slightly through the skin. When newly sloughed the scales have a metallic sheen reflecting all the colours of the rainbow.

Some geckoes are distinguished by very special defensive behaviour: shedding skin because of shock. Several herpetologists have been astounded when catching *Geckolepis* to find that instead of having a gecko in their hands, all they have is a few pieces of skin. This method of defence is unique in the animal kingdom, i.e., casting-off the entire skin, and not, as one would at first expect, only the epidermis at the point at which they are handled. This unique behaviour is made possible by special cells (a double layer of connecting tissue) which form splitting zones comparable to the breaking zones on the tail. This shock-shedding does not cause any injury because of the enormous powers of regeneration of these animals.

In spite of the total loss of skin there is only very slight bleeding at the point of "injury", and even after only a few hours a new layer of fine protective skin has formed. The skin needs around 3 weeks to regenerate completely.

If an animal is injured through shock-shedding in the vivarium, moist hiding places should be provided so that the animal does not dehydrate.

If the animals are handled regularly this behaviour ceases. To date this behaviour has been observed in the genera *Geckolepis, Ailuronyx, Teratoscincus, Aristelliger*, and *Phelsuma*, and is thus not limited to animals with one type of scalation.

COLOURING

When the word "gecko" is mentioned, thoughts immediately turn to grey or brown lizards which run around at night on the walls of houses in southern European holiday resorts. Only very few people think of the attractive and strikingly coloured *Phelsuma, Naultinus*, or *Gonatodes* species to mention only a few.

Almost all geckoes are in a position to lighten or darken their colouring. This is caused mainly by the dark pigment melanin passing into the melanin cells. If the melanin is contained in the lower part of the pigment cells the animals are lighter in colour, whilst when the melanin is in the upper part of the cells the animal becomes darker. This simple light-dark colouring has several functions. Darker animals absorb heat rays better than lighter coloured animals. Most frequently, however, the animals use this function to blend in with the background so that they are less noticeable. The colouring can also be an indication of temperament or condition, and it serves as a means of communication amongst themselves (submissive colouration).

The bright colouring of members of the genus *Phelsuma* is caused by pigment cells (chromatophores). These lie above the melanophores and cause essentially yellow or red colouring. In addition to these colour cells, the colourless guanophores provide the blue tones. The colour is caused by the guanophores reflecting and transforming light in such a way that as a result of light dispersion of certain wavelengths the colour blue is produced. If above the guanophores there is a layer

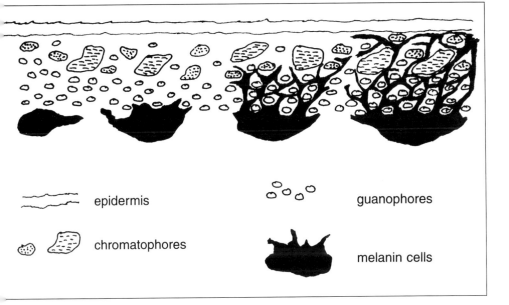

epidermis

guanophores

chromatophores

melanin cells

Schematic representation of the colour changing mechanism.

of yellow chromatophores, this gives rise to the colour green. The actual change of colour comes about as a result of a complicated interplay of individual colour cells. The most dramatic change of colour can be seen in *Phelsuma andamanensis*. During the day these animals are bright green with red markings, whilst at night they are almost totally black. It is also worthy of mention that patches of regenerated skin will no longer have the original colour.

GECKO FEET: SHAPE AND FUNCTION OF THE CLINGING MECHANISM

The construction and appearance of the toes and fingers of geckoes are so different that Boulenger (1885) attempted to compile a survey of the family Gekkonidae using these characteristics as a basis. In the names of the genera, fingers and toes are called "Daktylos" in Greek. This is Latinised as "dactylus" enabling immediate distinction because of the toes. Using some of the generic names which are still valid, we wish to show how the construction of the toes can simplify the relationship to a certain genus.

Blaesodactylus	=	Spread-Fingered
Carphodactylus	=	Thin-Fingered
Chondrodactylus	=	Granular-Fingered
Coleodactylus	=	Shield-Fingered
Crendactylus	=	Notch-Fingered
Cyrtodactylus	=	Curve-Fingered
Diplodactylus	=	Double-Fingered
Gymnodactylus	=	Naked-Fingered
Hemidactylus	=	Semi-Fingered
Hemiphyllodactylus	=	Semi-Leaf-Fingered
Holodactylus	=	Scale-Fingered
Lygodactylus	=	Twig-Fingered
Pachydactylus	=	Thick-Fingered
Phyllodactylus	=	Leaf-Fingered
Pseudothecadactylus	=	False-Fan-Fingered
Ptyodactylus	=	Split-Fingered
Rhacodactylus	=	Web-Fingered
Saurodactylus	=	Lizard-Fingered
Sphaerodactylus	=	Ball-Fingered
Thecadactylus	=	Fan-Fingered

The most obvious and impressive characteristic of geckoes is the ability of most species not only to cling to vertical and overhanging surfaces, but also to move around on them at great speed. They are able to achieve this because of the adhesive pads on the fingers and toes. Mankind has always been fascinated and astounded by this ability. It is therefore no great wonder that numerous myths have built up around geckoes, but it is interesting to note that two entirely different conceptions have arisen. On the one hand they are regarded as harbingers of luck, good fortune, and fertility, as is the case with the Tokay Gecko in parts of Southeast Asia. On the other hand they are regarded as venomous, as is the case in southeast Europe. In this way the scientific name *Tarentola* was derived from the poisonous Tarantula. Locally, *Hemidactylus turcicus* is called Tarantula. In parts of Madagascar *Uro-*

platus is classed as a devil, and should one be found hanging asleep on a hut in the early hours of the morning, the hut is immediately burned.

Numerous scientists have attempted to explain this unique quality. It was only in 1968 however, using pictures taken by an electron-microscope, that Hiller was able to recognise the fine structure of the minute bristles on the feet and was able to explain their function through various tests which he devised. The bristles, like the upper layer of skin, consist of dead keratin cells which are densely packed into the feet pads and which have the appearance of hairs. Viewed from above it can be seen that these clinging bristles are overlapped and arranged like roof tiles, in such a way that the end of one hair never lies beneath the previous hair and can always be seen as visibly free. At the end of each clinging bristle there is a characteristic bend pointing towards the root of the foot.

The actual arrangement can only be seen when greatly magnified under an electron-microscope. It can be seen that the end of each clinging bristle is split into several parts. These parts do not end uniformly, but at different distances whereby the final part results in the end structures. These end structures are only 0.2 μm wide and of varying lengths. The end of each shows a plate-like enlargement of 0.2 to 0.3 μm diameter which is deeper from the centre towards the edges. The end plates almost all lie on one plane which, because of the curve of the bristles, lie almost perpendicular to the longitudinal axis of the toes.

The question now is, how exactly do the geckoes stick and why do the clinging bristles have such a complicated structure? Hiller found the answer through tests during which he allowed geckoes to move on different surfaces each with a different surface tension. He was able to determine that the power of adhesion increased in proportion to the surface tension which signified that the clinging mechanism functions according to the physical principle of adhesion.

Adhesion means the sticking together of different bodies as a result of the molecular forces of the surface molecules or atoms. These forces are however only effective in extremely close proximity. That the adhesive forces are at all effective is guaranteed by the complicated structure of the individual clinging bristles. It is their microscopically fine structure which makes it possible for the geckoes to obtain the neccessary close surface contact for the pulling forces to become effective. The clinging capability is thus the sum of the infinite number of minute forces which become effective when the end structures of the clinging bristles come into contact with the surface below them.

That this clinging capability is purely a physical process is proved by the fact that dead animals do not lose their ability to cling and can remain suspended on a pane of glass. Because hanging in a perpendicular position does not require the expenditure of any energy, this is also the preferred sleeping position of many geckoes.

The only remaining question is therefore how geckoes put this clinging process into action and how they afterwards loosen their feet from the surface to which they have been clinging. For this purpose the feet are constructed in a way which makes them very flexible.

The actual clinging process results from a gripping action in the direction of the substrate during which, by means of muscular contraction, the clinging hairs are somewhat erected and pressed against the surface below them. By this means the clinging hairs assume an approximate 'S' shape bending towards the root of the foot. Because of the uniform positioning of all clinging lamellae the actual clinging force is thus only effective in the direction of the root of the foot. So that the animals are not helpless against forces from other directions, the toes are distributed almost equally around the foot giving the gecko a sure hold on the surface beneath it. To loosen the hold on the underground the toe is lifted from the front in a sort of rolling action. This process is carried out so quickly that it is almost impossible to observe exactly. By lifting the toes from the front the clinging hairs are progressively relieved and thus the adherent forces interrupted. After being released the clinging hairs spring back to their original position and the foot can be put down again. To lift a complete foot, i.e., to release all end structures at the same time, requires a great expenditure of force, a characteristic which they have at their disposal.

The clinging capability of some species of geckoes is enormous and is quite adequate to support several times their body weight. This is also neccessary to guarantee the animals a sure hold when jumping from one object to another.

Similar clinging hairs or other primitive clinging mechanisms can also be found on the tails and bellies of some species of geckoes. Even

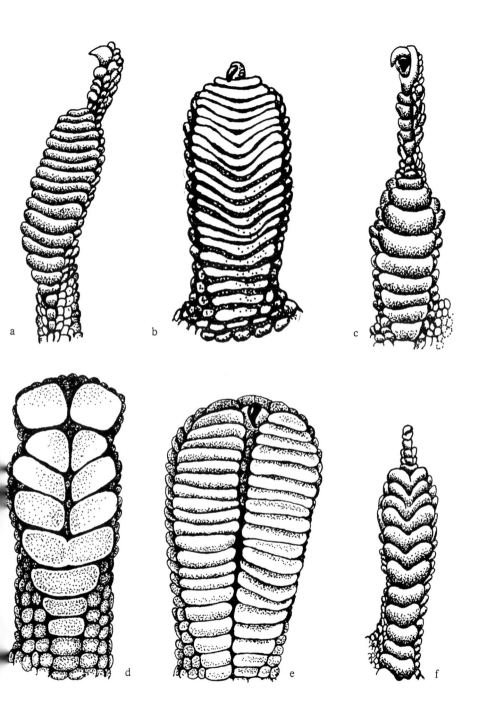

The multiplicity of gecko toes permits them to be roughly allocated to individual genera: a) Aristelliger lar. b) Gekko vitatus. c) Cyrtodactylus brevipalmatus. d) Oedura marmorata. e) Pseudothecadactylus lindneri. f) Hemidactylus garnotti.

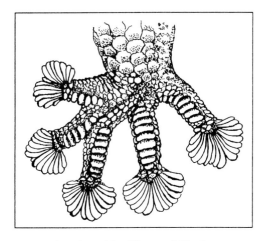

Foot of the genus Ptyodactylus—Fan Fingered Gecko.

inside the egg, the clinging hairs are fully-developed and protected by a thick layer of skin. This prevents the clinging lamellae being fouled during the hatching process. Soon after hatching the young geckoes slough, after which they possess their full clinging capability.

The clinging capability is at its strongest immediately after sloughing and steadily decreases until the next slough as a result of fouling of the clinging hairs. Because the new skin surrounding the hairs is more difficult to remove than normal skin, the gecko must take an active part in the sloughing process by removing this skin using its snout and mouth. Any residual skin on the foot of a gecko can have a very detrimental effect and in some cases the animal is unable to catch its prey and will thus starve to death. Residual skin on the foot of a gecko is often an indication that the animal is ill or weak.

Around each clinging pad there are also sensory cells which are situated exclusively on the perimeter scales. For example, *Tarentola mauretanica* has 15 sensory cells on each of these scales. These cells serve as feeling organs which cause the gecko to withdraw the foot should it come into contact with a liquid or sticky surface. In this way the adhesive pads are not fouled. Moreover, the sensory cells control the toes in relation to one another and supervise the clinging process.

The biological significance of this clinging capability is that it enables geckoes to live in habitats which are inaccessible for other rep-

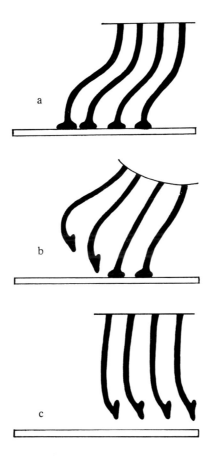

Schematic representation of the course of movement of the individual clinging hairs: a) clinging, b) loosening, c) released from underground.

tiles. Thus most species with clinging pads live on vertical surfaces
such as rock faces, tree trunks, and even on smooth palm leaves. Geckoes can also jump well and can hunt for prey on overhanging surfaces.
Many species make use of the protection offered by a vertical wall and
even use these as mating places. The clinging pads also permit geckoes
to become followers of civilisation, enabling them to live on bare walls
and ceilings.

Phylogenically, the development of the clinging lamellae did not run a uniform course. Whilst in most species the clinging hairs are primary, in some species they have reverted to a secondary function. At the present time around a third of all species have such a clinging mechanism.

It is when climbing or walking on rough or fissured surfaces that the claws come into play. Almost all species have well-developed claws. Using these gives the geckoes a firm hold on a surface where the adherent forces would be less effective, as is the case on tree bark or rough rocks. It is the ground-dwelling species which are especially dependent on their claws for digging and moving around. In these situations clinging hairs would be more hindrance than help and are usually not present.

There are two types of claws, fixed and retractile. In most arboreal species the claws are simply placed at the end of each finger and toe.

The grip of the claws is released in a similar way to the clinging hairs, by lifting the ends of the toes. When moving on a very smooth surface many species with clinging lamellae raise the claws. Animals of the genus *Uroplatus* can move their claws forwards and sink them below the clinging pads.

A further speciality of some sand and desert-dwelling species should also be mentioned: These are comb-like fringes and spiked scales which prevent the animals from sinking into the sand.

A special peculiarity has been developed by *Palmatogecko rangei* and the closely related *Kaokogecko vanzyli* and the convergently developed *Stenodactylus arabicus*. These species have webbed feet enabling them to walk easily on loose sand or bury themselves to escape from the sun or from animals which prey upon them.

GECKO TAILS: THE VARIOUS SHAPES
AND AUTOTOMY

Special mention must also be made of gecko tails, which have a wide variety of shapes and functions. The significance of the variety of shapes has not yet been explained.

In most cases the tail is simply elongated and round, tapering towards the end. In many species the tail is somewhat flattened on the sides. Other species have very short tails, whilst still others have cone-shaped tails. The genus *Nephrurus* has a cone-shaped tail which has a swelling at the end. This swelling is somewhat reminiscent of a button. For this reason they are given the common name of Button Tailed Gecko. Still other species, as in the genera *Uroplatus* and *Phyllurus*, have leaf-shaped tails.

As well as having a multitude of shapes, gecko tails also have many functions. These begin with simple coordination of movement when walking, climbing, or jumping. In many species the tail serves also as a clinging or grasping organ. When climbing, many gecko species anchor themselves by the tail. The clinging hairs on the tail are similar to those on the toes. Many species only have very weak clinging capability because in their case the structure of the clinging hairs is in transition between simple hairs functioning as claws and the very complex clinging hairs on the fingers and toes. The clinging apparatus is always at the end on the inside of the tail. The main purpose of this primitive clinging apparatus is to keep the tail horizontal to the body when the gecko is climbing on a vertical surface. The complicated clinging hairs fulfill the same function as do those on the feet. They serve to give the gecko a firm hold whilst climbing amongst branches.

The movements of the tail are equally important as a means of communication, especially amongst diurnal species. The tail movements are also an important part of the mating behaviour. For this reason some species of gecko have a different colour at the end of the tail, like *Gonatodes fuscus*. Other species have combs on the upper side of the tail, whilst some also have them on the underside (*Pristurus*), thus magnifying the optical significance.

Some species of gecko use their tail as a food reserve; most store this food in the form of fat. These reserves are stored for use during the winter or summer rest period. Geckoes from desert areas also often have a reserve of fat in their tail. This is stored for times when food is in short supply.

This explains why in the vivarium some geckoes frequently become obese. This is due to the fact that in times of plenty in the wild they lay down these reserves of fat. If such "greedy" geckoes are kept in the vivarium and fed regularly they will become too fat and only very rarely will they be able to use up these large reserves. When keeping these geckoes special care must be taken when feeding them, and in some cases a strict diet should be introduced.

As well as these basic functions, the tails of other geckoes have assumed other, more specialised functions. Thus the leaf-shaped tails of *Uroplatus fimbriatus* and *Phyllurus cornutus* serve primarily as camouflage. The wide flaps of skin on each side of the tail help it to blend into the background, thus making the animals "invisible." By rubbing its large tail scales against one another *Teratoscincus scincus* can produce a rattling noise which will sometimes deter an attacker. Using its short thick tail *Diplodactylus conspicillatus* can even seal its burrow in the ground so that no other animal may enter.

Like some other lizards, all geckoes have a remarkable defence reaction. They are in a position to actively cast off the tail and regenerate a completely new one. For this autotomy process each gecko tail contains several places at which it can break off. These are not between the vertebrae of the tail as would initially be thought, but take the form of hollow spaces in the centre of some basal tail vertebrae.

Thus if a gecko is seized only by the tail, the tail is cast off at the relevant breaking point. This process is carried out actively and does not depend upon the amount of force applied by the aggressor. In some species this process can be triggered by only very slight pressure being applied to the tail. The cast-off portion of the tail continues to wriggle violently for several minutes before slowing down and eventually stopping. The biological explanation for this manoeuvre is that the violently twitching tail distracts the aggressor, allowing the gecko to escape.

The capability of autotomy is developed to varying degrees amongst various species. Whilst some species will cast off the tail at the slightest pressure, others will only do so when violently molested. These are usually species which use their tail as a gripping or clinging organ, such as some *Rhacodactylus* and *Naultinus* species. A special mechanism ensures that once the tail has been cast off, the bleeding ceases very quickly and the wound heals rapidly. After a period of around 10 days, the regenerate begins to grow. Although the regeneration capacity is enormous, the new tail rarely reaches the length of the original. The scalation and patterning are also different from the original tail. Regenerates are usually unicoloured. The skeletal reconstruction of the regenerate is cartilaginous, and the autotomy reaction still functions, but only when autotomy occurs above the first breaking point.

In the wild it can often be seen that almost all animals of a given population have regenerated tails from which it can be measured how important autotomy is for the survival of the animals. However, tails can also be cast off during infighting within a group.

THE EYE

The most important sensory organ for a gecko is the eye, because it is by sight that they orientate themselves, especially when searching for food.

The most obvious part of a geckco's eye is the pupil, which, when closed, can show the most divergent patterning. Whilst in some species only a very narrow vertical slit can be seen in the middle, in some species the pupils overlap leaving at most four (very rarely more) holes, thus enabling the animals to see whilst their eyes are "closed." Earlier it was assumed that these holes in the pupil served as residual light intensifiers. It was assumed that the picture seen through the holes was projected several times over, thus forming a sharp picture in the gecko's eye even in half light. Seufer (1985) contradicts this thesis and it can be refuted by every herpetologist who has observed these animals carefully. If the animals are observed in the evening, when they are at their most active, it can be easily seen that the darker it becomes, the wider the pupils are opened. This shows quite clearly that as is the case with other animals, the pupils control the amount of light which enters the eyes, thus protecting the very sensitive visual organs from too much light. This is because many geckoes like to bask in the sun or inhabit the climates where they are forced into limited activity for part of the day.

As well as slit pupils there are also round pupils which are only found amongst diurnal geckoes. The shape of the pupil thus also gives an indication of the lifestyle of the animal. Those which are active at dusk or during the night always have slit pupils whilst most diurnal species have round pupils. Some species which have only recently

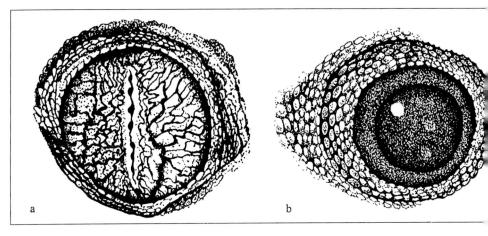

Various forms of the pupil in gecko eyes
a) Slit pupil.
b) Round pupil.

developed into diurnal animals still have slit pupils, e.g., *Ptyodactylus hasselquistii.*

Like most vertebrates, geckoes also have lensed eyes which permit pictorial sight. Responsible for the actual sight is the net skin, i.e., the light sensitive weave of the eye. The net skin consists of various layers: an outer, strongly pigmented layer; a layer of vision cells; and several other layers of nerve cells and fibres. In vision cells a distinction is made between two types, each of which has a different purpose. The cones make it possible to see in daylight and to distinguish colours, and the rods permit sight at dusk or night. The cones are the original form of visual cells; during the course of evolution the rods developed from them. Underwood (1954) examined the composition of the visual cells of numerous gecko eyes and arrived at the following conclusion: Most gecko species have evolved from diurnal into nocturnal animals and some species back again to diurnal animals. He distinguishes thereby two sorts of diurnal geckoes. The first are primary day geckoes, the subfamily Sphaerodactylinae, and the second are the secondary day geckoes to which the genus *Phelsuma* belongs. This is also shown by other characteristics.

Whilst most nocturnal geckoes are unable to distinguish colours because of the absence of cones, this is not neccessary for their life-styles. Day geckoes can however distinguish colours. What would otherwise be the purpose of a male *Gonatodes albogularis* having a bright red throat to threaten a rival or impress a female? This is also the case with Phelsumas. When attempting to impress a female the male lies on his side displaying the magnificent colours on his back.

During the course of time the cones of night-active geckoes have developed into rods which, like the split pupil, show an adaptation to activity at dusk or during the night. As a result of the pure-rod net skin, nocturnal geckoes (i.e., gecko species which are active after dark) are well able to detect shapes, outlines, and movements even with reduced light.

The difference between nocturnal and diurnal eyes can also easily be seen by the way the prey is caught. A nocturnal gecko will wait until its prey moves before seizing it. The opposite is true of a diurnal gecko (i.e., gecko species which are active during the day) which is able to recognise and catch unmoving prey.

The eyelids have also been transformed during the process of evolution. Whilst the original geckoes of the subfamily Eublepharinae (Lidded Geckoes) still have moveable eyelids, those of other geckoes have fused together and become transparent. It is interesting to note that in Lidded Geckoes the lower eyelid always moves upwards. The fusing together of the eyelids protects the eye from injury in the way that spectacles would.

On the top of the head, geckoes have the rudiments of a third eye. This now consists only of nerve ends in the upper layer of skin. It is suspected that its only remaining function is to coordinate activity to light conditions.

VOCALISATION AND HEARING

One of the special peculiarities of geckoes is their ability, unique amongst reptiles, to vocalise. This ability is not as well developed as in other vertebrates or birds, but it can nevertheless be compared to theirs. Not all geckoes have the ability to produce sounds. For example, the entire subfamily of Sphaerodactylinae is incapable of producing sounds.

The sound is produced from the lungs and the larynx which in some species creates an actual voice. In most species the call is monosyllabic but there are species which can call in several syllables. The nocturnal calling is best heard amongst human habitation since it is here that geckoes go hunting for insects and disputes frequently occur. It is under such circumstances that the southeast Asian species *Gekko gecko* was given its common name. Its call sounds like "to-kay" whereby it is now universally known as the Tokay Gecko.

The calls can be variously described according to species as chirping, croaking, piping, hissing, clicking, and barking. Some of the most imposing calls are those of *Cyrtodactylus peguensis* which is somewhat reminiscent of a canary, and the defensive call of *Uroplatus fimbriatus*. The call of this species is so loud that it can be heard in a neighbouring room. The barking call of an entire colony of Barking Geckoes of the genus *Ptenopus* is also an unforgettable sound.

A unique method of sound production amongst geckoes belongs to *Teratoscincus scincus* when it is molested. By rubbing together the scales on its tail it produces a rattling sound. If this does not cause the attacker to flee then the gecko itself attacks, producing a loud hissing noise.

There are many reasons for these calls. The first is obviously so that the geckoes may communicate amongst themselves. Whilst day geckoes have an optical solution which supersedes the function of calling and their call is only rudimentary and used as a warning signal, e.g., *Lygodactylus*, in nocturnal geckoes the call is the main form of communication amongst members of the same species. The calling of an entire colony of Barking Geckoes, for example, represents them proclaiming their territory.

Amongst other species the call is a way of finding members of the opposite sex during the breeding season and is part of the courtship procedure. The call further serves as a means of defence. Apart from all members of the subfamily Sphaerodactylinae, almost all geckoes will emit a hissing or croaking noise when molested.

This short summary only serves to show that almost nothing is known about the significance and composition of sounds produced within the family of Gekkonidae, and it is hoped that this method of communication will soon be thoroughly investigated scientifically using sonograms.

Because the call plays such an important role in the life of nocturnal geckoes, the acoustic sensory organ must be correspondingly well-suited to the perception of sound waves. The ear of a gecko fulfills the task of being a static and acoustic sensory organ and is built in the same way as the ear of other vertebrates.

Measurements of the hearing range showed that *Coleonyx variegatus* can hear from 300 to 1000 Hertz, whilst other species can hear sounds up to 10,000 Hertz. The ear is externally visible as a small hole on each side of the head.

THE ENDOLYMPHATIC CALCIUM SACS

Here a further organ must also be mentioned, the significance of which for the family of Gekkonidae cannot yet be sufficiently explained: the calcified endolymphatic sacs. These glands lie above a ductus endolymphaticus and are connected to the static organ. The calcium sacs lie in the lower throat and usually contain a milky calcium carbonate liquid. In the case of ground-dwelling chamaeleons of the genus *Brookesia* they serve as static organs by which the small chamaeleons in a condition of akinesis can always move with the stomach downwards thus presenting only the protected upper part of the body to a possible aggressor.

Such an explanation or observation and interpretation is to date not the case for geckoes. It is increasingly thought that the calcified endolymphatic sacs serve as calcium reserves enabling the females to produce hard-shelled eggs. In favour of this theory is the fact that amongst Gekkonidae they are only found in *Sphaerodactylinae* and *Gekkoninae*, and that they are absent in *Diplodactylinae* and *Eublepharinae*, which lay soft-shelled, parchment-like eggs. Against the theory however is that in some species the males also have endolymphatic sacs which do not contain calcium. Using X rays, Osadnik (1987) gave substance to the suspicion that the calcium sacs served as calcium stores for the formation of egg shells. Using *Phelsuma dubia* he was able to determine that the amount of stored calcium is significantly reduced during gravidity beginning on the 11th to 16th day after the last egg was laid and that whilst eggs are forming the amount of calcium builds up again. This storage mechanism prevents the female suffering enormous "calcium stress" whilst gravid, and simultaneously guarantees that sufficient calcium is available during the relatively short time in which the eggs are formed. There is even calcium in the endolymphatic sacs of embryos and newly hatched young. This calcium is vital to strengthen the skeletal bones of the young.

For the herpetologist it is important to know that without a balanced diet and with incorrect husbandry, these glands can easily become diseased. If too much calcium and vitamin D_3 are given these glands can harden. This can only be rectified by introducing a balanced diet and witholding calcium until the glands return to normal.

THE SENSE OF SMELL

The next organ to be considered is the nose, which as well as having the obvious function of a breathing organ, is also the externally visible organ of smell. In addition to the nose, geckoes can also detect smells and scents using the Jacobson's organ. In the nose scents are detected by numerous sensory cells situated on a membrane in the nostrils. Within the family Gekkonidae the Jacobson's organ is much better and more complex than the sense of smell in the nose. Moreover, it is directly connected to the nervous system. The sensory cells in the Jacabson's organ are built similarly to those in the nose. During embryonal development the Jacobson's organ separates from the nose and forms its own attachment to the palate. The Jacobson's organ lies on the bottom of the palate.

Geckoes have a thick, fleshy tongue, which at first sight does not appear suitable for carrying scent particles to the holes in the palate. The movements of the tongue are not as rapid or as accurate as those of snakes or monitor lizards. Thus it is probably often not considered to be tongue-waving. Nevertheless, using the tongue, geckoes carry scent particles to the hole in the palate from whence they are transported to the Jacobson's organ by body fluids.

The case of which sense of smell is most important for geckoes has not yet been investigated. Observations in the vivarium show that geckoes usually smell their food, especially fruit, using the nose, and only vary rarely lick it. In comparison however, recognition of the opposite sex is usually carried out by tongue-waving. This can easily be seen during courtship when the more advanced the courtship ritual, the more frequent the licking becomes. In this respect some authors speak of a threatening lick.

Because all nocturnal geckoes mate during the night, almost nothing is known about their licking during courtship.

A further example of using the Jacobson's organ is licking when searching for a suitable place to lay eggs. This is done by most females. Some scientists are of the opinion that the Jacobson's organ serves to identify newly caught prey.

Finally, it should be said that the combined sense of smell is only complementary to the sense of vision.

ACTIVITY AND TEMPERATURE REGULATION

Geckoes, like all reptiles, are cold-blooded animals. This means that unlike mammals and birds they are unable to keep their body at a constant temperature. They are dependent upon climatic conditions, primarily upon their immediate environmental temperature. The climate is thus the decisive factor for their distribution.

Because only very few regions of the world have constantly favourable climatic conditions which enable geckoes to survive, they have had to develop a whole series of mechanisms which allow them to regulate their temperature. The first is melanin, the colour by means of which the animals go dark in order to better absorb the rays of the sun, and by means of which fewer of the sun's rays are reflected. As well as becoming darker, most animals can also flatten their bodies, offering the largest possible surface area to the rays of the sun.

It is not only day geckoes which bask, but also many of the nocturnal species. These can often be seen basking during the early hours of the evening, so that their preferred temperature is reached before the onset of darkness. In the temperate zones, normally nocturnal geckoes can frequently be seen basking during the day when the weather is cool. After dark, other species lie on rocks which have been heated during the day. This behaviour now leads to many animals lying on the road at night, since the dark asphalt holds heat especially well. Inevitably, many geckoes and other reptiles fall victim to traffic whilst they are "topping-up" their heat reserve during the night.

If it becomes too warm for the geckoes they will retreat into their cooler hiding places. Usually these are holes in the ground, below loose tree bark, or deep crevices between rocks. Some species burrow into loose sand. This behaviour can be easily observed in the wild with day geckoes, which have two activity periods during the day. The first is in the morning when the animals have reached their preferred temperature, and the second is late in the afternoon when the hottest part of the day is over. This behaviour is rarely seen in the vivarium, in which temperatures are kept almost constant.

If geckoes are unable to find a cooler hiding place they will attempt to reduce their temperature by panting open-mouthed. This behaviour is normally only seen in the vivarium and is very rare in the wild. If it becomes even warmer still, the point will soon be reached when the animal will die from overheating. In the extremely hot desert regions, at the hottest time of the year, there is also usually a shortage of food, causing the animals to undergo a summer rest period in a cool hiding place.

Newly hatched and young geckoes are especially susceptible to death from overheating because the mechanisms for temperature regulation are insufficiently developed and their smaller organs quickly succumb to the higher temperatures. Most accidents occur because it is very easy to underestimate how quickly small rearing containers become too hot for survival.

To survive in the temperate regions geckoes must be able to hibernate in a frost-free place. However, even in the tropical regions many geckoes undergo a sort of hibernation or non-active period, for example, the geckoes of the eastern highlands of Madagascar which rest from the end of May until the end of August. This is the time between the monsoons when the temperatures are quite low.

TERRITORIAL AND DEFENCE BEHAVIOUR

With geckoes we are dealing with very fast, agile, and adaptable lizards. Around 75% of all known gecko species are active at night whilst some 25% are active during the day. Because of these different lifestyles there is a whole series of triggers for various types of behaviour, but also very divergent patterns of behaviour.

Basically, all geckoes are hunters. They either try to surprise their prey with a quick burst of speed before capturing it in their mouths, or they move very slowly and stealthily towards their prey in the manner of chamaeleons before seizing it suddenly. Day geckoes spend most of their period of activity basking, hunting prey, and defending their territory. Nocturnal geckoes too spend much of their activity period hunting for food, defending their territory, and, when necessary, seeking out warm rocks or similar places to maintain their preferred temperature. From this it could be thought that the behavioural patterns of these animals which are active at different times of the day are quite similar, but when more closely observed, considerable differences can be seen. Day geckoes, or at least *Phelsuma dubia*, have been thoroughly investigated by Osadnik (1987). However, there has still not been any in-depth research into the behavioural patterns of the majority of nocturnally active species.

What is particularly obvious in all gecko species is their pronounced territorial behaviour. They will defend their territory against intruders of the same species, but also to some extent against intruders of other species, thus ensuring less competition for food. In tropical countries, the peaceful scene of a number of geckoes gathered around a lamp is deceiving. When more closely observed it can be seen that there is a distinct distance between each animal. If this space is violated a fight invariably results. It is only the abundance of insects at such places which induces the geckoes to reduce their territorial demands for a short time. Soon after the light is extinguished the geckoes return to their normal territory and revert to their normal territorial behaviour.

Whilst day geckoes can be easily seen to exhibit extreme territorial behaviour, there is a whole series of nocturnal geckoes in which this behaviour is not so extreme, or in some cases even absent. In these species it can be seen that they remain at a certain minimum distance from one another. Some species only claim a distinct territory during the breeding season.

In almost all species the territory is claimed and defended by the male, but in many species the females also exhibit pronounced territorial behaviour. This is usually most obvious during the breeding season. If there are several females in the same territory there is usually a distinct order of dominance which is restated daily by biting. The dominant female occupies the best feeding place and is usually the first to mate with the male. In extensive observations, Osadnik (1987) found that in *Phelsuma dubia* both males and females defended their territory. This behaviour is also typical of other species.

A phenomenon which had previously only very rarely been observed amongst geckoes is the formation of permanent partnerships. A number of species appear to form a partnership whereby should one of the animals die the remaining partner will not normally mate with another. This is particularly true of *Phelsuma standingi*, a species which always occurs in true pairs on trees in the thorny savanna region of Tulear in Madagascar.

If older males or females are caught and an attempt is made to house them with another partner, this usually leads to a bitter fight resulting in the death of one of the animals. In younger animals this behaviour is not so pronounced, and they can therefore usually be introduced to new partners. Similar behaviour was also observed amongst the large *Rhacodactylus* species. Earlier, the occasional male or female reached Europe, but it was not possible to introduce them to one another. It was only when true pairs began to reach Europe that successful breeding occurred. This behaviour is however an exception since in most gecko species males and females can usually be introduced to one another without any great problems.

As well as species which live together as pairs or in small colonies, there are also species which live a totally solitary lifestyle and which only encounter the opposite sex during the breeding season.

In geckoes aggressive behaviour is very pronounced, as can be seen from the way in which they defend their territory. The greatest aggression is between males of the same species, although females will fight without any great provocation. There are even different patterns of behaviour towards younger animals. Some geckoes will eat all small lizards, even their own young, whilst others will chase their young from their territory. Still other species will tolerate their young in the territory until they reach sexual maturity.

Until quite recently there was the opinion amongst herpetologists that species which have a ringed pattern on their tail would not be eaten by their parents. There are indeed species for which this holds true, but unfortunately there are also a great many species which are quite prepared to eat their own young. It is therefore always advisable to rear young separately from adults, except in cases where it is known for certain that the adults will not molest the young.

The final section of this chapter will deal with the brood-protection-behaviour shown by some species of geckoes.

The behaviour towards geckoes of other species is also quite variable. Closely related species and those which have a similar appearance are much more likely to be threatened and chased from the territory than others which are externally different. Some species are extremely tolerant and can be housed with other species, even with other lizards. In the wild, several species are frequently found on one tree, but these usually have a different activity period or live in a different part of the tree, i.e., on or beneath the bark. Other species only have common sleeping places, for example beneath loose bark, but hunt for food in various biotopes; one on the ground, the other on tree trunks.

An excellent indicator of temperament is the tail. With a little practice, the mood of the gecko can be easily determined from the way the tail is moved.

What then are the individual differences in the behavioural patterns of nocturnal and diurnal geckoes? Because of the divergent activity times and varying degrees of light at those times, the behaviour of day geckoes is strongly influenced by optical triggers whilst that of nocturnal geckoes is triggered acoustically. Thus in day geckoes the ability to make sound is not at all pronounced, as is the case in the subfamily Sphaerodactylinae, or only present in a very rudimentary form, as in the case of *Phelsuma* species.

Because the behaviour of day geckoes is dependent upon optical triggers, these species are usually brightly coloured or have at least brightly coloured parts of the body. Only females and those species which have recently evolved into day geckoes have the remnants of inconspicuous camouflage colouring.

As an example, we wish to give a short description of the aggressive behaviour which Osadnik (1987) observed amongst *Phelsuma dubia*. If a male *P. dubia* strays into the territory of another male of the same species he will immediately be threatened by the holder of the territory. In this process two patterns of behaviour, each serving the same purpose, can be distinguished. The differentiation results from the position which the defender of the territory adapts in relation to the intruder. In the first instance the intruder is threatened from the front with the defender moving his body in the direction of the rival at the same time arching the back and turning the flanks to the side. In this way the male is attempting to appear larger, thus posing a greater threat to the intruder. The second process is the so-called threat from the side. For this the defender places himself at right angles to the intruder, whilst simultaneously flattening his sides. During both procedures both animals show their most beautiful and imposing colours. The defender will then run towards the intruder in a threatening manner, with jerky movements, head-bobbing, and the tongue flicking out. It is the latter action which indicates the importance of the Jacobson's organ. This is used not only to detect a sexual difference, but also to identify a true partner. This has been proved in several tests. During this threatening process the animals continue to flick out the tongue. This has probably little to do with threat and serves more to identify the intruder. If the defender is now close and the intruder shows no signs of fear and is also making threats, this invariably leads to a fight during which the males will attempt to bite one another and push one another backwards. Usually, the intruder will retreat before actual bites are inflicted. However, if it does come to a short fight, it is interesting to note that it is almost always the territory defender who wins.

For herpetologists the significance of this is quite easy to see. In small or medium vivaria, *Phelsuma* species may only be kept in pairs or in groups of one male with several females, otherwise the dominant male would constantly threaten and attack his subordinate, who is unable to escape because of space limitation. The subordinate male would thus eventually be so weakened that death would result. Attention must also be paid to females during their first days together because they too can sometimes be very intolerant of one another. *Phelsuma dubia* females will also threaten other *P. dubia* females which intrude into their territory. If the threat alone is not successful these females are much more ready than the males to engage in a serious fight. In some species it has also been seen that pairs will act in unison to defend their chosen territory.

The males of some *Gonatodes* species exhibit especially pronounced threat behaviour. These males usually have a brightly coloured head and throat. The animals watch over their territory from the highest point and threaten any lizard which comes near by frantically bobbing the head and inflating the throat. By inflating the throat the males, like many *Anolis* species, make their head appear larger and more imposing to an opponent.

The behaviour of nocturnal geckoes is quite different. Optical signals would be quite useless to them in marking their territory. They were thus forced to develop acoustic signals as a replacement. Many nocturnal geckoes therefore delineate their territory by loud calls which warn an intruder not to come nearer. The most imposing of all territorial calls must surely be that of an entire colony of Bell Geckoes.

If another male does penetrate the territory a fight usually results much more quickly than it would with day geckoes. As far as threat behaviour is concerned, to date only head bobbing and hissing have been observed. Regarding nocturnal geckoes, it can only be said at present that as is the case with day geckoes, there are tolerant and less tolerant species. Because their activity period only begins after the lights have been extinguished, it is very difficult to make any exact observations of the threats and other behavioural patterns of nocturnal geckoes. This therefore presents an interesting and challenging field of research which unfortunately no one has yet accepted.

Even after only 3–4 days young animals already possess the entire programme of fighting behaviour. Because these young are often intolerant of one another, as well as the young of other species, it is advisable that the young of many species be reared individually. To anyone seeking more exact details on the behaviour of day geckoes, the works of Kästle (1964) and Osadnik (1987) are highly recommended.

Special care should also be taken when breeding some of the live-bearing species. It has been known for male *Rhacodactylus trachyrhynchus* to eat their own young soon after birth.

Normally *Rhacodactylus trachyrhynchus* live in pairs on enormous trees in the jungles of New Caledonia. In all probability the female gives birth in hollows in the trees and defends the young from the males and other predators for a certain time after birth. When the brood protection of the female ceases, the young have developed a pattern of behaviour unique amongst geckoes: They escape into water. In the vivarium the young hide in the water contained in the reservoirs of bromeliad plants, where they submerge completely. They remain there motionless for several minutes before slowly raising their snout above water level. At the slightest disturbance they immediately submerge again. This pattern of behaviour is also exhibited when they are disturbed by humans.

The general pattern of defence behaviour of geckoes against an aggressor varies widely. Whilst well-camouflaged species always rely on their camouflage and only move when they are touched, other species try to prevent themselves being molested by very rapid movements.

At this point mention must also be made of the autotomy of the tail and emergency skin-shedding. These are factors which have undoubtedly contributed towards the survival of numerous gecko species.

Many species emit loud calls when molested. The most impressive and loudest call is the defensive call of *Uroplatus fimbriatus* which sounds like a cat that has had its tail trodden on.

Of the many divergent patterns of behaviour exhibited to deter enemies, that of *Teratoscincus scincus* serves as an excellent example. If it feels threatened *T. scincus* produce a rattling sound caused by rubbing together the rough scales on its tail. If this is not sufficient to deter the enemy, it will attempt to threaten by raising its body and emitting loud hissing and barking noises before finally charging at its aggressor and biting. Anyone who has observed this behaviour in the vivarium can well imagine that in the wild most attackers would be deterred.

Equally interesting is the defensive behaviour of *Chondrodactylus angulifer*. This species sets itself up against an opponent by raising its body and curling its tail over its head. In this way the animal bears a great resemblance to a scorpion. This optical imitation of a dangerous insect is underlined by the gecko hissing loudly at its attacker.

To be able to determine whether parents defend their own young or carry out brood protection, several tests were undertaken:

In a large vivarium the eggs of a pair of *Gekko gecko* were left until they hatched. The eggs were protected by the parents. When the young hatched they were also guarded by the parents and left in peace. At this point it should be stated that the Tokay is a species which will happily eat small lizards and is not selective when choosing which species to eat. Some days later the young were removed from the parental vivarium and after a further few days were reintroduced. They were immediately devoured. The broad protection ended when the animals were separated and even the ringed tail did not protect the young from their parents. It would appear that recognition of their own young results not optically but in all probability from the sense of smell and the Jacobson's organ.

HOW LONG CAN GECKOES LIVE?

This is a very difficult question and one which is not easily answered. Too many factors play a decisive role. There is also a considerable difference between life expectancy in the wild and in the vivarium, with the most favourable expectancy being in the vivarium. How the animals are kept in the vivarium can also easily prolong or shorten their life. Absolutely vital for most animals is that in the vivarium they should also be able to have a resting period similar to that dictated by the climate in the wild. For information, some examples are given below:

Species	Life expectancy in captivity
Coleotzyx variegatus	ca. 14 years
Eublepharis macularius	ca. 22 years
Gecko monarchus	ca. 10 years
Gonatodes fuscus	ca. 7 years
Oedura tryoni	ca. 15 years
Phelsuma madagascariensis grandis	ca. 20 years
Phyllodactylus europaeus	ca. 22 years
Sphaerodactylus nicholsi	ca. 12 years
Tarentola mauretanica mauretanica	ca. 20 years
Most small *Phelsuma* species	ca. 7 years

Anyone wishing to keep geckoes should always remember how long these animals can live and the length of time one will be responsible for their welfare. It should also be borne in mind that improved knowledge of husbandry and ever increasing scientific knowledge will probably mean that geckoes will live even longer in captivity in the future.

Reproduction

In this chapter we wish to illustrate in detail all aspects of reproductive behaviour.

Successful breeding in captivity is of paramount importance due to constant environmental destruction, which leads to ever-increasing habitat losses for geckoes. Even today it is quite imaginable that in the very near future some rain forest species will no longer have a natural habitat in the wild and that the most highly specialised of these species will become extinct—if they are not already extinct in the wild.

For herpetologists, therefore, the most important problem at present is the correct care of the animals in captivity and the successful breeding of these species. Even now it can be forseen that in the near future numerous species of geckoes will only be able to be found as captives in vivaria.

Since there will be no possibility in the future of taking animals from the wild, selective breeding in the vivarium is vital so that as the breeding programme progresses there are no signs of degeneration. This begins immediately after the young have hatched. Any young which are unable to free themselves from the egg using their own strength should not be given any assistance since they will undoubtedly be too weak to use for future breeding programmes. Once the young have hatched or been born, any which show signs of deformation or any undersized animals should not be used for breeding.

An ideal situation would be a selection system similar to that used by Schröder (verbal communication) with his animals. He always rears each species separately and seeks out the strongest for future breeding. In this way he has already bred *Paroedura pictus* to the F_{16} generation (Schröder, 1987) and no doubt at the present time has even bred further generations without any signs of degeneration. Many herpetologists have had similar successes with other species.

Equally important as the selection of the animals to be used for breeding is the establishment of the largest possible breeding group of suitable animals, because a shortage of unrelated genes can also critically affect the resulting offspring. This can only be avoided if working groups of interested parties are formed, thus establishing the largest possible gene pool. This is now happening regularly with more and more species. It is more important to keep one or two more animals of each species than to keep one animal from each of 10 species. Specialisation and the investigation of the demands and lifestyles of these animals are of vital importance and are urgently required for their future survival.

SEX DETERMINATION

An important prerequisite for breeding is that the sexes of the animals to be used are correctly determined. There are various characteristics which enable males and females to be distinguished. The first is a difference in colour. This colour dimorphism is very pronounced amongst day geckoes, and is at its most significant amongst animals of the genera *Gonatodes*, *Lygodactylus*, and *Quendenfeldtia*. In these species the males are much more brightly coloured than the females, e.g., by having a brightly coloured head. Even amongst some *Phelsuma* species the males are easily distinguished from the females by their more vivid colours.

As well as the differences in colour the sexes can sometimes be distinguished by means of the body proportions. In some species the males are larger and much more robust than the females. This is best seen by comparing the shape of the heads on animals of equal size. In other species, males, as opposed to females, have small retractile claws on the toes of the hind feet. Moreover amongst the individual species there are numerous differences which can be discovered by comparisons.

In a male one of the most obvious sexual differences is the slight swelling at the base of the tail. This swelling is caused by the two hemipenes which lie concealed in two skin pockets. This characteristic is quite significant and is easily seen in almost all species. Equally easily seen are the preanal and femoral pores (thigh pores) as

Foot of the genus Ptyodactylus—Fan Fingered Gecko.

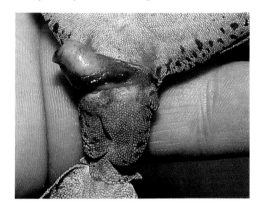

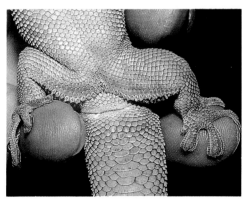

Centre: Extruded hemipenis of Uroplatus fimbriatus.
Below: Preanal pores of Phelsuma m. grandis.

well as the postanal tubercles which are much more strongly defined in the males. The preanal and femoral pores produce a yellowish, sticky secretion, the significance of which has not yet been investigated. It is however suspected that these pores produce scent particles which are used to delineate territory. The postanal tubercle is to hold open the female cloaca during copulation.

A good indication of sex can also be indicated by the behaviour exhibited, depending upon whether the animal is showing threat behaviour or courtship behaviour.

As well as these externally visible characteristics there are a whole series of methods to determine the sex of a gecko, but these are only of limited use to the average amateur herpetologist. The simplest of these is by using a piece of cast-off skin, because even the skin of the hemipenes is sloughed regularly and on the old skin the ball-shaped swelling near the opening of the cloaca can be easily seen. With a little practice and experience the hemipenes can also be massaged until they become visible.

Other possibilities are probing and hormone determination. These methods are often used on other reptiles when the sex of the animal is not externally visible. Unfortunately these methods are rather expensive and on smaller species can only be carried out to a limited extent and with some danger of injury.

ADDITIONAL PREREQUISITES FOR BREEDING

If one now has a guaranteed pair the following must also be taken into consideration: Have they already reached sexual maturity? This is reached at a different age from species to species. When reared under favourable conditions some species can reach sexual maturity at the age of only 6 months whilst other species such as *Rhacodactylus leachianus* are not sexually mature until the age of at least 5 years. The size of the individual species is also no criterion since *Gekko gecko* for example is mature at around 9 months. Young from the same clutch may also not all reach sexual maturity at the same age. For species which breed throughout the year it is thus advantageous when the males are somewhat older than the females. If given a choice, captive-bred animals should always be selected before wild-caught specimens. This is not only because of the possibility of illnesses and parasites, but also because the exact age of the animals is also known. Several species live for some years after they have ceased reproducing.

When initially introduced to one another care should be taken that the animals get on well together. It sometimes happens that certain pairs will not tolerate one another and should be separated after a few days if losses are to be avoided.

A very important factor for breeding species from the temperate regions is the observation of the reproductive cycle because in the wild many species have an annual cycle of reproduction. This means that the animals will only breed after the ending of winter hibernation or the end of the dry season. The cyclical variations or rather the maturing of the gonads are firmly allied to these reproduction times.

For herpetologists this poses the following question: Which are the triggering factors for reproduction? There are various triggers. The most important is the annual cyclical temperature variations since in reptiles an increase in temperature causes an increase in the metabolic rate. This in turn activates the nervous system in such a way that it triggers the start of the reproductive cycle. As well as the temperature, the photoperiod is also an important factor in some species. By photoperiod, the constant annual dark-light ratio is meant, or expressed in another way, the constantly changing length of the daylight hours. If one wishes to hibernate species from the temperate regions, the period of light and the temperature should be gradually reduced. As well as these factors, for tropical species there is also a certain dependence on the seasonal rainfall. Many species begin their annual reproductive cycle at the start of the rainy season. This is very expedient because it is at this time when there is usually an abundant supply of food in the form of insects.

The best prerequisite for finding a suitable partner is a high population density and it would appear that most gecko species have realised this because they come together in very large numbers in one biotope. Because of their diminutiveness and the scattered lifestyle of some species, geckoes must develop a whole series of signals for finding members of the opposite sex. It is much easier for the day geckoes because they, or at least the males amongst them, have vivid colours and are easily visible. Thus the animals are more easily able to find one another for mating. This behaviour is best observed amongst males of the *Gonatodes* species, which survey their territory from above, carefully watching all lizards which enter. This is greeted by threat behaviour, which promptly changes to courtship behaviour should a female enter the territory. The varying patterns of the individual species prevent them from mating with the wrong partner. This means of species identification does not appear to present any difficulties to the animals in the wild. Since in vivaria species are often kept together which do not encounter one another in the wild, now and again mismatings occur, resulting in cross-bred young. It is possible that the animals would mismate in the wild, but because of their spatial isolation this is most unlikely. Mismating can also occur as a result of over-stimulus when the animals are living very closely together. In the vivarium this frequently means the effective end of a certain species because the resulting young are inevitably infertile, making back-crossing very difficult.

After optical identification, of which appearance and behaviour are a part, there is also olfactory (scent) recognition when the animals are in close proximity to one another. Only then does mating occur in the wild. Although in some areas of Madagascar numerous *Phelsuma* species occur in one biotope, mismatings are unknown in the wild.

Nocturnal geckoes must develop a completely different series of signals which enable the sexes to locate one another. The most important characteristic is once again the call. Using the call, the males delineate their territories and attempt to entice the females into them. The importance of these calls and whether mating would actually take place without them has still not been explained. It would appear quite certain, however, that other species have developed still other methods of finding a suitable partner, because in the vivarium they never utter any territorial or courtship calls. Even in the wild these animals manage to find one another to mate, despite enormous distribution ranges. In all probability this is achieved by means of the Jacobson's organ, with which, like snakes, they are able to detect the most minute scent particles.

As well as these possibilities the geckoes have developed still other strategies to ensure pure breeding. Advanced fertilisation, also known as sperm-storing or amphigonia retardata, is worth mentioning as is the asexual reproduction (parthenogenesis) which will be considered later. Here mention must be made once again of the formation of true partnerships. The species which have been seen to form these permanent relationships all live in one distinct territory or biotope in which no animals of the same species will be tolerated. The individual territories are usually well separated within a large distribution range. The chances of large *Rhacodactylus* species finding suitable partners during the breeding season would otherwise be very small since they are normally only found on one species of tree, the next example of which could be a long distance away. The same could also be said of other species which live together as pairs.

REPRODUCTIVE BEHAVIOUR

There are only very few accurate observations of the patterns of courtship and reproductive behaviour of geckoes so that here we must relate our own observations which were for the large part made on day geckoes.

If a male day gecko detects another gecko of the same species, the intruder is immediately threatened. If the male realises that the other animal is a female the threat behaviour is promptly replaced by courtship behaviour. Because both patterns of behaviour are very similar, a threatening courtship is frequently spoken of. Using jerky movements, the male approaches the female, while at the same time exhibiting his enlarged-flank threat behaviour. This can be compared to the aggressive behaviour. Other behavioural elements such as head bobbing and tail waving have not been observed and would thus not appear to be part of the courtship displays of day geckoes.

If the female is not ready to mate she has several ways to deter the male. Some females shake the head wildly which discourages the male. Others make sudden pseudo-attacks on the male or approach him with sideways movements and simultaneous head shaking. This behaviour usually has the desired result of causing the males to discontinue their courtship display. However, the display is usually resumed a short time later. It is only after he has met with several refusals that the male desists completely. In a small vivarium in which the female cannot get out of sight of the male, the constant pestering by the amorous male can often lead to reciprocal biting. This aggressive behaviour is intensified even further during gravidity. In such a case the animals should be separated until shortly after the eggs have been laid.

If, however, the female is ready to mate, she at first pays no attention to the machinations of the amorous male. Using jerky movements the male approaches the female. If she continues to show no signs of defensive or aggressive behaviour, he finally begins to touch her at the base of the tail, or at least in that area. In some species the male will even inflict a gentle bite on the hind thigh.

It is only amongst *Phelsuma* species that we have been able to observe excessive licking. Even during his initial approach the male begins licking and whilst climbing over the female this licking becomes even more frantic. In this case, some authors speak of "threat-licking." In our opinion this has nothing whatsoever to do with threatening behaviour. We are of the opinion that sexual scents excite the male and encourage the licking. This explains why the licking becomes more and more frantic the closer the animals are together. Because the nocturnal geckoes of the subfamily Sphaerodactylinae do not exhibit this behaviour it would appear that in *Phelsuma* it is a relic from when they were nocturnal species.

The *Phelsuma* male climbs over the female several time before finally biting the neck and placing his cloacal opening below that of the female. Whilst the male is climbing over the female both animals move their tail from side to side, enabling the male to place his tail more easily beneath that of the female. During some matings the female tries to move a few centimetres forwards. So that the female is not able to escape and to ensure that the hemipenes are not damaged by jerky movements, the males of many species hold the female in position by biting her firmly in the neck region. This bite is held throughout copulation which can last up to 30 minutes.

Not so many details are known about the mating behaviour of nocturnal geckoes. In some species the males attract the females by their territorial calls. With the non-calling species it can only be supposed that the sexes find each other by means of scent particles or by increased mobility during the mating season. As soon as visual contact has been established the nocturnal geckoes behave in almost the same way as day geckoes. Tail waving, head bobbing, and sideways movements have all been seen to be part of the courtship behaviour. For the actual mating the male also approaches the female from the rear. In the vivarium mating usually takes place in the evening.

In some species no courtship behaviour has been observed. In these species matings take place almost by surprise. How important a part of the mating behaviour the call is has not yet been explained, but it has been seen in certain species that the females answer the males, and that the sexes call to one another regularly, e.g., *Cyrtopodion kotschyi*.

ADVANCE FERTILISATION AND GRAVIDITY

Whilst gravid, the female usually becomes more aggressive. This is directed towards the male and other females. It is important that at this time the female is not disturbed unnecessarily. It is also vital that they are given a balanced diet and an adequate supply of vitamins and minerals. At this time some females of some species will also eat calcium, although they do not normally do this. It is therefore advisable to place a bowl of powdered cuttlefish bone in the vivarium.

Because of their lifestyle and the difficulties sometimes encountered in finding a suitable partner, the females of almost all species of gecko are in a position to store sperm in the oviduct for a considerable period of time. They can therefore lay several clutches of eggs from only one mating. It is probably because of this function that they are now distributed worldwide.

The sperm is stored in the receptaculum seminis, a long, tubular, branched gland which lies near the shelling gland in the oviduct. When and how the eggs are fertilised from there has not yet been investigated. The first sperm can be found in the receptaculum seminis around 14 days after the initial mating.

OVIPOSITION AND BIRTH

Within the family of Gekkonidae there are two different types of reproduction: oviparous—the laying of eggs, and ovoviviparous—the bearing of fully-formed live young. The first type of reproduction is the normal case, whilst the second is known only from a small number of species such as the New Zealand geckoes of the genera *Heteropholis*, *Hoplodactylus*, *Naultinus*, and the New Caledonian Giant Gecko *Rhacodactylus trachyrhynchus*. As far as the New Zealand species are concerned this represents an adaptation to the relatively cool climate which prevails throughout the year. The female can thus individually select the most suitable temperature for the development of the young, for example by basking. The production of live young by *Rhacodactylus trachyrhynchus* represents an adaptation to its arboreal lifestyle.

If the birth process of live-bearing species is closely observed, it can be seen that it is not the typical birth process of live-bearing animals. It is more a case of fully-developed young being produced in a calcium-free protective sac from which they immediately free themselves using violent stretching movements. This is thus not described as an incubation period but rather as a pregnancy period.

The much more common form of reproduction is that of laying eggs, a process which has been observed many more times than the birth of live young.

If the eggs are about to be laid this is immediately apparent by the behaviour of the female. Some days before laying the eggs the female searches for a suitable laying-site. This is recognised by the restlessness and constant movement of the female around the vivarium. Shortly before laying the female will go to the selected site and may remain there for several hours. This pronounced searching activity proves that the female is checking very carefully to find the optimum place for the successful development of the eggs.

How carefully the females seek out a suitable place to lay their eggs can be seen from the number of mass-laying-sites which are known from several species. If a female of one of these species has a choice of suitable places, she will invariably choose the place where eggs are already present. Tests have shown that a female can easily determine whether eggs which are already present have been damaged, whether there are signs of development, and whether the eggs have been disturbed. This method of selection has the advantage that the eggs are laid in a place which is well-protected from predators (Osadnik, 1987).

Geckoes which lay soft-shelled eggs are those of the subfamilies Diplodactylinae and Eublepharinae. The eggs of these species have a protective coating somewhat reminiscent of leather, and must therefore always be buried in moist substrate to prevent them from drying out.

For species which lay hard-shelled eggs the situation is much simpler, but they too must take certain precautions. Although the eggs are minerally encrusted and thus protected from drying out or other mechanical influence, it is important that the eggs are laid in an optically well-protected place so that the eggs, which are normally pure white, do not become immediately obvious to other creatures which would eat them. Some species which lay hard-shelled eggs have thus developed a special process to protect the eggs. Shortly before the calcium shell has hardened completely the eggs are rolled on the ground so that particles of earth, sand, etc. adhere to them so that the eggs assume a camouflage colouring making them less conspicuous.

Even in the case of day geckoes the eggs are usually laid during the evening or at night under the cover of darkness, which makes the laying site more difficult to find and prevents the females from falling prey to other animals which would eat them. In many species the females remain close to the clutch until the eggs are completely hard and thus protected from mechanical damage. During this time the female will chase away any other gecko which approaches the eggs (see Territorial and Defence Behaviour).

The composition of gecko eggs is similar to that of other reptiles. An egg consists of an embryo surrounded by an amniotic sac. Also inside the egg there is a large supply of yolk contained in a yolk sac, the allantois in which the metabolic products are stored, and the chorion which lies directly below the shell. The shell consists of a "typical squamata", parchment-like casing in the case of soft-shelled eggs, or a hard calcified shell in the case of hard-shelled eggs.

The development of the eggs until the hatching of the young is called embryonal development. During this time the allantois combines with the chorion, forming the chorio-allantois. This absorbs oxygen through the shell of the egg and releases carbon dioxide from the egg. In an incubator containing many eggs it is therefore vital to en-

Female Phelsuma m. grandis in oviposition.

sure adequate ventilation at all times. As opposed to hard-shelled eggs, which can no longer alter their shape during development, soft-shelled eggs, by absorbing moisture from their surroundings, continue to expand until shortly before hatching. In the case of hard-shelled eggs, the darkening of the shell is usually an indication that the egg is fertile and developing. Infertile eggs usually retain their yellowish sheen, whilst soft-shelled eggs usually collapse after a few days.

That hatching is about to begin is signified in soft-shelled eggs shrinking and the surface of the egg becoming moist. This is the so-called "sweating." Soon afterwards, using its egg tooth, the hatch-

A unique occurrence. Uroplatus henkeli with a clutch of four intact eggs.

ling makes a longitudinal incision in the shell. It later emerges from this incision. In some species the young split only the end of the egg to enable them to hatch.

In the case of hard-shelled eggs the young usually cut a hole in the shell which is then split during the actual hatching process. The egg tooth is usually lost during the neonate slough soon after hatching. It is only after this neonate slough that the young have the ability to cling to smooth surfaces.

In most gecko species the clutch consists of two eggs. It is only the *Sphaerodactylinae* and other small species which normally produce only one egg per clutch. Nevertheless some other species have been known to produce only one egg occasionally.

The eggs are generally spherical or ovally elongated in shape and, depending upon species, can vary in size from 3 mm to 45 mm.

A great deal has already been written about the various ways in which eggs are laid, and according to some authors, geckoes which have clinging lamellae on their feet do not bury their eggs. However, vivarium observations on numerous species of geckoes have shown that some species with clinging lamellae do indeed bury their eggs, whilst the majority do not. Even amongst the *Phelsuma* species there are those which bury their eggs, e.g., *Phelsuma guttata*.

Species which lay soft-shelled eggs always bury them. Other species lay their eggs in rock crevices, beneath tree bark, in hollows in trees, at the forks of branches, in the funnels of plants, on leaf joints, or in other secluded hiding places. Some species even affix their eggs to surrounding objects where they are held firmly in place by the calcium layer. To do this they press the newly-laid eggs firmly against the chosen object until they have completely hardened. *Phelsuma barbouri* attaches its eggs to overhanging rocks and uses its belly to press the eggs against the rock until they finally stick.

The egg-laying process of large *Phelsuma* species such as *Phelsuma madagascariensis grandis* can be easily observed.

This species lays two calcium-shelled eggs, the so-called "double clutch" which stick to one another. In the chosen laying site the female turns onto her back and lays the first egg. By using her hind legs she rotates the soft egg until it is almost spherical. She then lays the second egg which is also rotated until almost spherical before pressing it against the first and holding it there until they stick together. After both eggs have hardened completely the female then places them in the chosen hiding place.

An important exception to the soft-shell-producing Diplodactylinae is *Rhacodactylus chahoua*. This species does indeed produce soft-shelled eggs, but eggs which also have a fine coating of calcium. Because of this coating, this species, whether it knows it or not, can also produce a "double clutch". According to our observations, eggs which stick together do so only accidentally because most clutches consist of individual eggs. *Rhacodactylus chahoua* thus represents the transition from "typical squamata", parchment-like eggs to the more developed species which produce hard-shelled eggs.

During the breeding season most species have a laying cycle of around 4 weeks between each clutch of eggs.

PARTHENOGENESIS AND QUESTIONS OF GENETICS

In the introduction to the chapter on reproduction we have attempted to answer the most important question on genetics, namely whether constant breeding in the vivarium eventually produces young which are either infertile or incapable of survival.

Here we wish to briefly reconsider the question of colour inheritance in species and subspecies hybrids. In some of the deliberately produced hybrids, but also in some of the accidentally produced hybrids it was shown that amongst the cross-bred subspecies there was a dominant recessive gene, at least as far as typical colouring was concerned. Cross-bred species amongst the genus *Oedura* proved to be fertile.

At this point mention must also be made of parthenogenesis. By parthenogenesis or virgin birth we mean reproduction from unfertilised eggs. This means that there are only females of a species or within a population. It is suspected that this method of reproduction arose through hybridisation. To date, parthenogenesis is known from only five species of gecko. The first of these is *Lepidodactylus lugubris* which is the only diploid species. No males of this species have been found. Within certain populations, four further species are known to reproduce parthenogenetically. These are *Hemidactylus garnoti*, *Gehyra variegata ogasawarisinae*, *Nactus arnouxii*, and *Heteronotia binoei*. The disadvantage of this method of reproduction is that all animals are genetically identical. The fact that the species *Lepidodactylus lugubris* and *Hemidactylus garnoti* are now so widely distributed can be explained on the one hand by the doubling of fertility in that there are only females, and on the other that the establishment of a population requires only one animal or one egg.

THE INFLUENCE OF THE INCUBATION
TEMPERATURE ON THE SEX
RATIO OF THE YOUNG

During recent years there has been considerable discussion regarding the predetermination of sexes by incubating reptile eggs at different temperatures.

This phenomenon is already known for several crocodile, tortoise, turtle, gecko, and agama species. Because the research in this field could have considerable significance for wildlife conservation and for herpetologist, a short survey of the present state of the art is given below.

Every herpetologist who regularly breeds several species of gecko and who incubates the eggs at different temperatures will already have determined that at a certain temperature only one sex will be produced, or at least there will be more young of one sex than the other. This phenomenon has been studied in much greater detail by Wagner (in Bull, 1980) and Osadnik (1987). The latter work is strongly recommended to any reader particularly interested in this phenomenon.

During temperature experiments in his laboratory, Osadnik found that the geckoes he was studying in depth, *Phelsuma dubia*, tended to produce more males when the eggs were incubated at higher temperatures. With *Phelsuma dubia*, temperatures above 30 °C will usually produce more male young. Lower temperatures produce more female young.

Further experiments in the laboratory produced the interesting result that if the temperature varies daily between 20 °C and 32 °C an almost equal ratio of males to females is produced. Tests in the wild produced similar results. At a mass-laying site at Mahajanga, Osadnik measured temperature variations between 23.5 °C and 32.2 °C and was able to determine that when the young hatched this resulted in a sex ratio of 1:1.

The observation that the sex ratio is dependent upon the incubation temperature has been proven by our own observations on numerous other species. It would appear to be true of all *Phelsuma* species, for *Eublepharis macularius* and other species of the genera *Uroplatus* and *Ptychozoon*. There are almost certainly other species to which this principle would apply. Unfortunately, most gecko keepers do not record the sex ratio of any resulting young and usually do not associate this ratio with the incubation temperature. For this reason reports are only very rarely published, making it impossible to compare species with a temperature-dependent sex ratio. King (1977) proved that it is possible to determine sex using chromosomes.

With the phenomenon of temperature-dependent sex ratio it is interesting to note that this appears to be purely a laboratory "problem", because variations in the wild always provide an equal and neccessary sex ratio. It is only the "sterile" incubation temperatures in an incubator which cause a "problem" with temperature-dependent sex ratios.

Anyone breeding geckoes must ensure that an equal sex ratio is produced and not only males or only females.

An important factor for breeding success is the knowledge that the sex of the young is probably determined during the first one-third of the incubation period, and that all observations to date, even with other lizards (e.g., *Agama agama*, Charnier, 1966) indicate that a higher incubation temperature produces more males whilst a lower temperature produces more females. Where the borderline lies must be experimentally determined for each individual species. It is quite possible that for some species the opposite is true or that for the production of one particular sex even two temperature ranges may be necessary.

If this phenomenon is considered in total and compared to other vertebrates, it appears to be a problem which is peculiar to reptiles and the historical purpose of which has not yet been investigated or explained.

From this short discussion it can be seen that there are still countless aspects which must be investigated scientifically. We hope that this method of sexual determination will soon be examined in detail so that it may be used in nature conservation projects as is already the case with marine turtles, where, by producing more females, it is hoped to be able to increase the reproductive quotient.

The Vivarium

As is well known, several gecko species are covered by international wildlife protection treaties.

SPECIES PROTECTION

The first wildlife protection treaty was the Washington Agreement which regulates international trade in protected and endangered species. As a result of the Washington Agreement, the gecko species *Phelsuma* and *Cyrtodactylus serpensinsula* are now protected. This means that in practice these species may only be sold when accompanied by a CITES certificate. This is a sort of "Identity Card" for animals. This certificate has been required since 1st January 1984. Every responsible herpetologist should only purchase animals accompanied by the necessary papers. These papers must be available for inspection by any recognised wildlife protection authority and should therefore be kept in a safe place. Breeding successes or the death of the animals should be reported to the relevant authority within 4 weeks.

According to our extensive observations, geckoes are not really rare creatures, but because of their rather secretive lifestyles are usually difficult to find.

Many species, amongst them *Phelsuma*, have evolved to become followers of civilisation and many species live in large numbers on plantations. In our opinion, species protection is only sensible when at the same time the habitat of the species in question is also protected. The species which are most endangered are those highly specialised jungle and rain forest dwellers which are losing more and more of their habitat each day, and species which inhabit small islands. Protected status for these animals is vital and urgent.

GECKOES IN THE VIVARIUM

Because of the large number of gecko species it is natural that they do not all inhabit one type of habitat, but rather that they have adapted to a number of different climates and biotopes. This has significance for vivarium husbandry. The husbandry conditions can be very divergent depending upon the origin of the animals. They depend also on the requirements and adaptability of the species being kept.

If the Gekkonidae family is compared with other groups of reptiles frequently kept in captivity, it can be said that geckoes are usually undemanding and easily kept animals which are also relatively easy to breed. They are thus especially recommended for keeping in captivity.

Most species can be easily housed and cared for without a great deal of time having to be spent on them. Some species are particularly adaptable and make only very small demands on the vivarium required to house them. However, a few ground rules should be observed so that the animals quickly settle in and begin breeding. An example of this is *Lepidodactylus lugubris*, a parthenogenic species which for laboratory purposes has been kept and bred over several generations in small plastic containers converted into vivaria.

As well as these flexible or non-specialised species, there are also a number which are tied to a particular climate or biotope. To be able to keep these highly specialised animals it is essential that their habitat be recreated as far as is possible under vivarium conditions. Some of these species inhabit rain forests, some deserts, and still others live in special climates, such as the geckoes from New Zealand.

When keeping these highly-specialised species, the keeper should also be warned that it is not absolutely neccessary to reproduce all conditions which can be found in the wild. It is both pointless and unneccessary to create a surface temperature of 50 °C or more in a desert vivarium or to install expensive spraying systems in a rain forest vivarium. A healthy average is the main prerequisite for successful husbandry and breeding. This does not mean that the neccessary temperature variations on an annual cycle should not be provided, only that the extemes of heat and cold should be avoided.

To provide the herpetologist with some guidelines for correct husbandry and breeding, the individual species descriptions of all subfamilies are grouped together into genera and given in table formation below. The tables contain data on distribution, typical habitat, and the most suitable type of vivarium for each genus. Using these tables, guidelines can also be obtained for the husbandry of species which are not contained in the section on individual descriptions. Further necessary information regarding the relevant climate can be taken from the appropriate specialist literature, e.g., Müller (1983). When using such generalised climatic data however, care should be taken because the data given will not always agree with the conditions prevalent in the special habitats. For example, the temperatures in the rain forests are frequently lower than in the surrounding areas.

POSITION OF THE VIVARIUM

When the decision has been made to obtain a vivarium, the question of where to position it should be given careful consideration. The most important factor to be considered is the temperature, which must remain within a certain range. The greatest danger of overheating a vivarium is from the sun, especially during the summer months. Even during winter care must be taken that the sun's rays coming through the window at a steeper angle do not penetrate into the vivarium. Especially in small vivaria it only takes minutes for the temperature to increase to such an extent that the animals die from overheating. The vivarium should therefore be installed in a place where it will only be in the sun during the early hours of the morning or late afternoon. In summer it can also happen that in a south-facing room or in an attic the temperature can soon exceed the permissible value which the animals can tolerate. It is therefore always advisable before placing the animals in the vivarium to carefully measure the temperatures. Espe-

Part of the reptile room of one of the authors.

cially suitable are north-facing rooms or a well-insulated cellar, because it is easier to heat a room than it is to cool it.

When keeping tropical species it is also equally important that the
temperature does not drop too low. This can easily happen in a conservatory or greenhouse. When keeping species from temperate zones
however, this can be advantageous because for hibernation the vivarium may simply be left in this room.

DO-IT-YOURSELF OR BUY?

The range of vivaria which are now available commercially is enormous. They can be bought in all shapes and sizes corresponding to the

Open vivaria for ground-dwelling species.

demands and requirements of their future occupants. Usually, containers purchased from shops are of standard sizes and cannot always be universally integrated, whereby special orders must be placed or a spot of construction is called for. Nowadays, a number of companies will manufacture vivaria to order. Their addresses can be found in specialist magazines or newspapers. Provided the neccessary tools and time are available, it is quite easy to build a vivarium using materials from the local do-it-yourself supplier. The simplest container is one made from panes of glass, stuck together with silicon sealer. Neither of these materials is harmful to geckoes and they present no problems when cleaning or disinfecting the vivaria. The glass needed to build such a vivarium can be obtained cut-to-size from the local glazier who will grind the sharp edges to prevent injury. It is even less expensive if the glass can be cut from old window frames. All silicon sealers are suitable fixatives. This material is manufactured from an acetic acid base. Directions for the construction of all-glass vivaria can be found in Nietzke (1978), Lilge and van Meeuwen (1989), and in numerous other publications.

POINTS TO CONSIDER WHEN PLANNING A VIVARIUM

It is often said that lizards have a great need of fresh air and this is indeed also true of some species of gecko. It is therefore important that totally enclosed containers have at least two ventilation panels. The most suitable arrangement is to have a ventilation panel on the front of the vivarium. This prevents condensation forming on the the the glass. This is particularly important in moist and rain forest vivaria since the front panel would otherwise be constantly wet, encouraging the growth of algae. Ventilation panels can also be fitted to the side or rear walls of the vivarium. The second ventilation panel should always be in the vivarium cover so that constant circulation of air is guaranteed and stale air can not be trapped in the vivarium.

In vivaria intended for species which require relatively high atmospheric humidity, the ventilation panels should be correspondingly smaller. Since it is very difficult to estimate the correct size of the panel, at the beginning it is best kept large. The area may then be suitably reduced using a piece of glass or foil.

In desert vivaria and those used for keeping species which require a great deal of fresh air, the ventilation panels should be as large as possible. This also creates low atmospheric humidity which is exactly the condition required for a desert vivarium.

If, for a certain species, good ventilation and high relative atmospheric humidity are required, then the movement of air must be provided by a small ventilator fan such as those used for cooling electronic equipment or computers. When keeping larger species which feed on crickets, locusts, or, other large insects, the adjustable ventilation panels should be made from metal gauze. The insects are quite able to chew through plastic mesh. Plastic mesh is however suitable for rearing containers and for vivaria to contain the smaller species of gecko.

Geckoes with clinging lamellae present something of a visual "problem" in that they appear to prefer the front glass panel as a resting place. Unfortunately they also appear to prefer the front glass panels as a place to defecate. A black-white speckled glass front presents no great problems if the vivarium is in a separate reptile room. If however the vivarium is the showpiece of the living room, this can be rather annoying. By using a suitable selection of plants with long smooth leaves such as Sanseveria, and by installing stout bamboo poles the geckoes can be attracted away from the glass towards the centre and rear of the vivarium.

One certain way to prevent the glass panel from becoming fouled is to install it at a slight angle (for instructions see Lilge & van Meeuwen, 1979). The geckoes will still cling to the glass, but the excrement falls to the floor from whence it is easily removed. An additional improvement provided by a sloping front panel is that in narrow vivaria it gives the impression of greater depth and thus appears more attractive.

The question of how large a vivarium should be for the correct husbandry of a certain species is often very difficult to answer. The correct answer depends upon several factors. In general it can be said that geckoes with clinging lamellae generally require smaller vivaria, or one with less volume, than other comparable species which do not use all available space as an activity area and generally tend to use only the walls of the vivarium to move around.

The following factors are decisive when determining the correct size of the vivarium:

1. The size of the animals. It is important that the supplier be asked how large the animals may eventually grow.
2. The temperament of the animals. Peaceful animals require less space than the more lively species.
3. The number of animals to be housed. It must be taken into consideration that four animals of the same species require more space than a pair each of two separate species.

4. The varying degrees of aggression of the various species of gecko to be housed. This is often very difficult to determine accurately. When kept in pairs in suitably large vivaria, many species will claim a territory. If more animals are introduced the normal territorial behaviour is sometimes subdued, giving the false impression that the animals are tolerant. This is no longer a case of correct husbandry, as will be recognised by the fact that the animals do not breed and never exhibit their complete behavioural pattern.

Other species are so aggressive that they will still claim a territory when there is insufficient space for the other occupants. The dominant animal will then threaten and attack all subordinates which have insufficient space to escape. This can cause stress and even the eventual death of the subordinate animals.

If several animals of a particularly aggressive species are to be housed together, each animal must have an individual basking place so that it may reach its preferred temperature without being molested by the dominant animal. Each animal must also be able to retreat to an individual hiding place which has a lower temperature. This is only possible in a very large vivarium. By suitably arranging the vivarium furnishings and plants, and by providing several heat sources and feeding places, several individual territories may be established.

As well as the dimension or volume of the vivarium, the shape also plays an important role when keeping geckoes. Ground-dwelling species should be given the largest possible floor area, whilst tree-dwelling species should be housed in a vivarium with the greatest possible height. For all vivaria with the exception of those for bush and ground dwellers, the depth is of no great importance since the animals usually make use of the vertical walls for their activity areas.

There is always danger when opening the vivarium. This is especially true when keeping geckoes with clinging lamellae. These species often cling to the front panel, and when the vivarium is opened they are often overlooked, allowing them to escape. The speed, agility, and fantastic clinging ability of geckoes should never be underestimated and caution should always be the keyword when opening a vivarium which contains geckoes . . . the loss of a tail could be only one of the minor consequences.

TYPES OF VIVARIA

Despite the fact that geckoes are extremely adaptable, various vivaria are required for correct husbandry. In the following we give five suggestions for various types of vivaria suitable for keeping geckoes. These five vivaria are only a very small proportion of the large number of containers currently available commercially.

There are species which require a combination of these types of vivaria. The five described could not possibly meet the requirements of every known species of gecko and only serve as guidelines. If two species are to be kept together, e.g., a tree-dwelling and a cliff-dwelling species, a combined habitat may be created if the vivarium is large enough. Species which have totally different habitats, e.g., desert and rain forest species cannot be housed together for obvious reasons.

The Dry Vivarium For Ground-Dwelling Species (I).

Ventilation: Open top or gauze cover.
Substrate: A layer of sand 3–10 cm deep. Part of the substrate should be kept constantly moist.
Furnishings: Rocks, roots, branches, pieces of cork bark for hiding places.
Plants: Not neccessary, but succulents may be used.
Species: Ground-dwelling or burrowing species which do not have clinging lamellae.

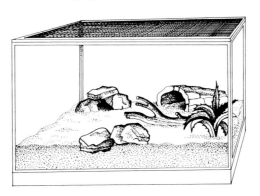

Vivarium type I: Dry vivarium for ground-dwelling species.

The Dry Vivarium For Cliff-Dwelling Species (II).

Ventilation: At the side and on top of the vivarium.
Substrate: A layer of sand 1–3 cm deep.
Furnishings: Flat rocks stacked against the rear wall in such a way
                that crevices are provided. Some flat rocks leaning
                against the side walls.
Plants: Not neccessary but succulents may be used.
Species: Geckoes which live on rocky cliff faces in the dry and
                desert regions of the world.

The Planted Vivarium (III).

Ventilation: On the side and top of the vivarium.
Substrate: A layer of potting compost or bark mulch 3 cm deep.

Vivarium type II: Dry vivarium for cliff-dwelling species.

Furnishings: Several pieces of hollow cork bark on the ground as
               hiding places. Several upright sturdy branches.
Plants: Any plants originating from the regions of the species
               to be kept.
Species: Geckoes which do not live in either deserts or rain
               forests.

The Rain Forest Vivarium (IV).

Ventilation: Small ventilation panels below the front glass panel
               and on top of the vivarium.
Substrate: A layer of potting compost or hydroponic culture
               balls several centimetres deep.
Furnishings: The side and rear walls should be covered with cork
               tiles or bark. Several stout, upright branches or some

Vivarium type III: The planted vivarium.

Vivarium type IV: The rain forest vivarium.

	stout bamboo poles which are especially suitable for *Phelsuma* species.
Plants:	Robust, bushy plants. In larger vivaria epiphytes, orchids and Tillandsia species can be attached to the stout, upright branches.
Species:	Geckoes from the tropical rain forests.

The Moist Vivarium (V).

Ventilation:	Small to medium ventilation panels (varies according to species to be kept) below the front glass panel and on top of the vivarium.
Substrate:	A layer of potting compost or hydroponic culture balls several centimetres deep.

Vivarium type V: The moist vivarium.

Plants: Decorative climbing or trailing plants.
Species: Geckoes which live on cliff faces in the sub-tropical
               regions.

FREE-RANGE GECKOES

Many herpetologists who keep reptiles and amphibians also have free-ranging geckoes in their reptile room, conservatory, or greenhouse. The main purpose of these geckoes is to catch escaped food insects and spiders which gather in such places. Because they are so very adaptable, those species of gecko which have become followers of civilisation are especially suitable for this purpose. The artificial conditions in the reptile room often approximate those in their natural habitat so closely that many species will soon settle in and start to breed. The animals often become very trusting and can be seen at all times of the day.

Before releasing geckoes into the reptile room however, several points must be borne in mind. The room must always be kept firmly closed to prevent escapes into other rooms or to the outside. If a window is to be opened for ventilation, the gap must be completely covered by a fine gauze. If European species are to be allowed free-range it must be remembered that these animals will also need somewhere to hibernate. If the reptile room is in the cellar or attic the geckoes will soon find somewhere suitable for hibernation. They will disappear in the late autumn to reappear again in the spring. The internal clock still functions although ideal conditions prevail in the reptile room. It is thought that this behaviour is influenced by the shortening hours of natural light. When the above requirements are met, breeding presents no problems.

A further point to be considered when keeping free-range geckoes is that the temperatures should always correspond to that prevalent during the natural activity periods of the animals. Naturally the temperatures vary from species to species.

In the average reptile room there are always adequate hiding places, each with a different temperature. There is however great danger in conservatories or greenhouses because these are subject to greater temperature fluctuations. Even with only a very brief period of sunshine they can soon reach the critical maximum temperature. On the other hand they must be uniformly heated to at least 10 °C. Thus special micro-climates must also be provided: in summer cool, moist hiding places; and in winter, heated places where the animals are able to reach their preferred temperature.

One of the disadvantages of keeping free-range geckoes is that the animals must also regularly deposit excrement. In a special room this again presents no problems. In a conservatory which is not used entirely for herpetological purposes however the constant fouling of the glass and furniture can be rather annoying. Because some species lead a very secluded lifestyle and also deposit their excrement in secluded places, tests should be carried out to determine which species is most suitable for the room in question.

Finally, feeding is also an important factor. There must always be sufficient food available. Many herpetologists have been amazed to find that animals which had been thought to be long dead from starvation suddenly turn up months later looking quite healthy and well-fed. At some time, however, the geckoes will have consumed all the wild insects and will need to be fed. This is best achieved by installing a feeding container from which the geckoes may serve themselves, but from which the food insects are unable to escape.

The selection of species suitable for a free-range lifestyle is however a little more difficult. As already stated, the most suitable species are those which in the wild have become followers of civilisation and can frequently be found inside houses in their countries of origin. Some of the most suitable species are *Hemidactylus frenatus*, *Hemidactylus garnotii*, *Hemidactylus mabouia*, *Cosymbotus platyurus*, *Gehyra variegata*, *Lepidodactylus lugubris*, and *Gekko gecko* amongst others.

THE OUTDOOR VIVARIUM

Many gecko species, especially those from the temperate zones, can be safely kept in an outdoor vivarium during the summer months. These species include those animals from Europe, Chile, and New Zealand as well as members of the genus *Afroedura* from South Africa. For all day geckoes and for many nocturnal species it has been proved to be advantageous on warm sunny days to give them a "summer holiday" outside in an outdoor vivarium. Suitable outdoor vivaria can be easily constructed from very fine mesh. It is vital however that there is no build-up of stale air and that the furnishings of the vivarium meet the requirements of the occupants. The vivarium should always be placed in a position where it is half shaded. It is only under these conditions when many day geckoes will show their most beautiful colours and their full behavioural pattern. The animals are also much more active. Moreover, the period in the outdoor vivarium usually acts as a stimulus for subsequent breeding. This is especially true of species which enjoy a great deal of light and sunshine, e.g., *Lygodactylus picturatus* and some *Phelsuma* species.

When keeping geckoes in an outdoor vivarium care must be taken that the containers are placed in a position where they are safe from the local cats and dogs. Shrews and other small predators can also present a danger, especially on cooler days when the geckoes are unable to reach their normal activity temperatures and are rather lethargic. It is then that they can easily fall prey to these small predators.

VIVARIUM CREATION AND FURNISHINGS

When furnishing a vivarium an attempt should always be made to re-create a section from the biotope of the natural habitat of the geckoes to be kept. Frequently the optical impression is the most important. However, this often does not agree with the actual conditions to be found in the wild and compromises must be sought. Who would wish for example to recreate a rubbish dump on which an animal was perhaps caught? On the other hand, the appearance of the most barren-looking desert can be improved by adding some attractive succulent plants.

The exact recreation of the natural biotope is not the most important aspect of furnishing a vivarium. It is much more important that the requirements of the animals to be housed in it are met. Suitable living conditions must be achieved but they need not be identical to those found in the wild.

The choice of substrate for ground-dwelling species is especially important. For most species which live in the desert and arid regions medium grade sand is suitable. Before being placed in the vivarium the sand must be thoroughly rinsed under running water. It has proved expedient to keep a section of the sand permanently moist. This can be separated from the remainder by strips of glass firmly fixed to the base of the vivarium by silicon sealer. This prevents the moisture penetrating to the dry section.

When keeping species from Australia or South Africa it is especially advisable to use red sand if this can be obtained. It is not only the typical ground dwellers (most of which have no clinging lamellae) which live on the ground, but also a multitude of other species, including members of the genera *Paroedura, Cyrtodactylus*, and *Sphaerodactylus* to name only a few. Amongst other places these species live along the banks of streams and on the forest floor. Many *Sphaerodactylus* live amongst leaf litter and in the loose humus layers on the forest floor. For these species the substrate should consist of a shallow drainage layer, a 2 cm layer of potting compost and a 1–3 cm layer of leaf litter. To ensure that the leaf litter retains its volume and does not begin to rot as a result of constant spraying, several pieces of cork bark and cork tile should be placed below it. Before being placed in the vivarium the leaves should be thoroughly washed and dried so that no slugs, snails, or centipedes are introduced into the vivarium. For other forest dwellers, one half of the substrate should be covered with dry leaf litter and the other with moss. Light flat rocks which will serve as hiding places should also be provided.

For planted vivaria the substrate should always consist of two layers; hydroponic culture balls or polystyrene beads for drainage and an upper layer of potting or forest compost, in the absence of which a sand/peat mixture may be used. Often in a rain forest vivarium only hydroponic culture balls covered by moss and leaf litter are used.

Since many species live on rocks, in rock crevices, and on stone walls, natural rock must also be used in the vivarium. Artificial cliff faces may also be easily created. Rocks are very heavy, requiring the base of the vivarium to be solid. It is essential if the vivarium is of the all-glass type that the base stands firmly on its support. Rock piles should always be built from the base of the vivarium and not from the surface of the substrate. The animals could otherwise burrow underneath and be crushed to death. If you intend to build an artificial cliff face into the vivarium, the rocks must not simply be laid one on the other. It is better if they are firmly fixed to one another. Using a model, the cliff face may be built in sections in such a way that each section may be easily removed so that each hiding place may be inspected. Before being used, the cement may be dyed to match the colour of the rocks. Before being installed in the vivarium, the cement parts must be thoroughly rinsed.

A convincing imitation of natural rack can also be made from polystyrene; a polystyrene sheet is broken into various sized pieces which are then stacked together to form a stone wall with crevices. Alternatively, using a soldering iron, a block of polystyrene can be "sculpted" to resemble a rock. Once this has been achieved, the entire construction is given a coat of external brickwork paint of a suitable colour. The finished article may then be sprinkled with sand or fine gravel and allowed to dry before being installed in the vivarium.

Many species require no substrate as such. The base of the vivarium is simply covered in sand or cork tiles. Many herpetologists have bred several generations of geckoes in vivaria such as these.

For species hailing from more moist regions, one or more potted plants should be installed. These should be kept permanently moist and the compost covered by pieces of cork tiles. This somewhat spartan and sterile method of gecko husbandry has many advantages. The vivaria are easy to clean and the arduous task of searching for eggs is simplified, because they will invariably be laid in the plant pots.

The coverings for the side walls should be chosen according to the requirements of the species to be kept. Thus for tree dwellers the rear and one side wall should be covered with cork. One wall should be left uncovered. This will possibly attract the animals away from the front glass panel and help to avoid fouling. When selecting cork several choices are available. The most attractive, but also the most expensive, is pressed natural cork bark which can be bought in several sizes. Somewhat less expensive are the 3 mm cork tiles used for internal decorating. Equally suitable are the cork tiles used for covering ceilings. These come in a variety of thicknesses from 1–5 mm and may also be used to form a landscape. Because there are two types of cork tiles, pressed and glued, the former must always be chosen because the latter are toxic.

For cliff-face dwellers the rear and one side wall should be covered with thin slices of natural stone. These too may also be given a coat of external brickwork paint of a suitable colour which is then sprinkled with sand or fine gravel.

For climbing, almost any branches or roots may be used. Since species with clinging lamellae prefer smooth branches, stout bamboo poles are especially suitable. A very picturesque effect is created when several upright bamboo poles are installed at the rear of the vivarium.

When installing hiding places attention should be paid to the required micro-climates of the individual species. Not only warm and dry, but also moist and cool hiding places should be provided. Hiding places can be in rock piles, below rocks, in burrows, in cork-bark tubes lying on the substrate, or in hollow chambers in bamboo poles into which access holes have been cut. A suitable imitation of tree hollows for large to medium sized species is commercially available nesting boxes for birds. These are easily opened for inspection and cleaning. Some species however prefer loosely suspended cork tubes or pieces of bamboo. The list of possibilities is endless and limited only by the imagination. It is important to take notice when the animals do not accept the retreats which are provided for them and wander restlessly around the vivarium, or when animals which are normally active at night are seen throughout the day. In these cases new retreats and hiding places must be provided.

The piece of vivarium furnishing which should never be overlooked is the water container. Even in a desert vivarium it should always be present!

PLANTS IN THE VIVARIUM

There are only a small number of gecko species which are as dependent on plants (with the exception of tree trunks) as the *Naultinus* species from New Zealand, so that plants are normally only used for decorative purposes. The main purpose of the plants should be an attempt to recreate the natural habitat of the animals as far as is possible. In the vivarium the plants help the animals to establish territories by preventing eye contact.

When making a selection, the needs of the plants must also be taken into consideration, and these should be similar to the needs of the geckoes. Only robust plants should be chosen. Plants such as Sanseveria with its long, narrow, smooth leaves are especially suitable for many gecko species. Moreover, Sanseverias are very hardy and easy to care for. Unfortunately, they are not as decorative as other plants. They should be placed at the rear of the vivarium to entice the geckoes away from the front glass panel.

When planting a gecko vivarium the lighting is also important. With day geckoes this presents no problems because they need as much light as the plants. It is however completely different for nocturnal geckoes, which only require very little light. If plants needing a great deal of light are to be installed in a vivarium containing nocturnal geckoes, then adequate lighting must also be provided. Finally, a word of warning. Before placing any plant in the vivarium it should be thoroughly rinsed to remove any trace of pesticide with which it may have been sprayed.

COHABITATION WITH OTHER ANIMALS

Basically, geckoes should be kept separately according to species. It will not bother them, however, if they are kept with other reptiles and amphibians as long as there is no competition for food. It is obvious that the animals should all share the same climatic requirements. The vivarium should also be large enough for the animals to avoid one another, although in general the geckoes will pay no attention to their cohabitants.

Many herpetologists who keep small diurnal animals such as Arrow Poison Frogs also keep a pair of nocturnal geckoes in the same container. It is their task to eat any excess food insects, which maybe too large for the smaller animals, or which may have remained hidden during the day. Geckoes should never be kept together with snakes. They have an inborn fear of their serpentine cousins.

THE BREEDING, INCUBATION, AND REARING OF YOUNG GECKOES

In the following section a summary is given of the most important prerequisites for breeding geckoes successfully in the vivarium.

The main prerequisite is that the animals are a true and harmonious pair which are not too old. If the animals are wild-caught it can be

quite some time before they finally settle in. The idea of buying geckoes one day and having eggs seven days later only occurs very rarely,
and even then only with the more "usual" species. This sometimes requires several years, therefore "patience" is the keyword. If there have
been no breeding results for an extremely long time an attempt should
be made to alter the conditions under which the animals are being
kept. It should also not be forgotten that many species have a very distinct breeding period.

If the mating has been successful the female must be particularly
well fed because she may have an increased food requirement. Further
problems can arise when the time to lay the eggs arrives. To prevent
difficulties in laying, several suitable places should be provided, giving
the female as wide a choice as possible. The ideal places to lay eggs or
give birth can be very divergent. For example, a simple pile of moist
sand, a potted plant in which eggs are easily buried, a bird nesting box,
or simply a hollow tube or a dark corner where eggs may be deposited
or attached. If a species is kept about which there is no knowledge concerning where it would normally lay its eggs, then several of the above
possibilities should be provided. It is also important that, whilst gravid,
the female should not be subjected to any stress, such as by being
moved to another vivarium or by introducing any new animals.

A special problem is posed by adhesive eggs. The female will attach
the eggs to the place she considers most suitable. The place where the
eggs have been laid must be carefully sought. This is easiest achieved
using a small mirror by means of which all corners and overhangs may
be investigated. Adhesive eggs cannot be removed from the vivarium.
Any attempt to do so will break them.

To prevent the eggs and the young from being molested by their parents or other vivarium occupants, and to avoid having to search for the
young in a large vivarium, the eggs should be covered by a transparent
plastic container which prevents any animal from approaching them
and which will limit the movements of the young when they hatch.
Naturally the plastic container surrounding the eggs should have a
number of small ventilation holes. If the geckoes have affixed their
eggs to a sliding glass panel this should be placed at the back so that
no other sliding glass can damage the eggs. With other species the eggs
should be immediately removed from the vivarium. The same applies

to newly born or unnoticed newly hatched young which should be reared in separate small vivaria.

Locating the eggs can often be quite troublesome. Nevertheless it must be done with great care so that the thin fragile shells are not damaged. The eggs should be removed from the vivarium without turning them and should be placed in small containers. Any tightly closing container with a transparent lid is suitable. The container should be filled with one of several suitable incubation mediums. For desert-dwellers slightly moist sand is reccommended and for all species with soft-shelled eggs only a moist medium should be used for incubation. The most useful and suitable medium is vermiculite which absorbs and holds moisture well. There are two types of vermiculite. One is available from builders merchants as an insulation medium and is treated, whilst the other is untreated and used for the cultivation of orchids. Only the latter should be used for incubating eggs.

Because young geckoes slough and eat the cast-off skin soon after hatching it has been known for them to also ingest minute particles of vermiculite and die. For this reason only the larger grade of vermiculite should be used. It should be thoroughly rinsed before use to prevent the accidental ingestion of any minute particles it may contain.

In the incubation containers there should never be excess water which cannot be absorbed by the vermiculite. Because different species require different degrees of substrate moisture and because the eggs absorb the moisture relatively quickly, the substrate should be checked at three-week intervals and further water added if neccessary. This also provides the requisite air exchange. The degree of moisture is increased by carefully spraying around the sides of the container. The eggs themselves should never be sprayed. If the eggs begin to show signs of mould this is an indication that they are infertile. They should be immediately removed and discarded so that the remaining eggs do not become infected.

Hard-shelled eggs are best incubated in a dry substrate such as sand or preshaped foam rubber. With the eggs of some species adequate relative air humidity must be maintained. This is between 60 and 80%. The eggs themselves however must never come into contact with any moisture.

No general statement can be made about the incubation temperature, but it should never exceed 32 °C. The lowest value is around 20 °C. In general, all eggs can be hatched at 25–28 °C. With some species it has been proved to be advantageous if the eggs are subjected to daily temperature variations; in these cases the young were more active. With species which bury their eggs there should be no variation in the temperature, since below ground the temperature remains almost constant. When incubating eggs the problems of temperature-dependent sex ratio (see page 54) should not be forgotten.

Any commercially available or self-constructed device (see Broer, 1978) is suitable for the incubation of gecko eggs.

Immediately after hatching or being born, the young should be transferred to separate rearing containers, which should be obtained and prepared well in advance. They should be miniature versions of the vivaria housing the parents. In many species with clinging lamellae and especially for rearing young *Phelsuma* species, transparent storage containers are suitable. As large a section of the lid as possible should be cut out and replaced with plastic gauze (ca. 500 μm) which is fixed in position by silicon sealer. One side of the container should also have a 3 × 5 cm gauze-covered ventilation hole some 2 cm above the substrate. The inside of the opposite side should be covered with a piece of cork tiling used for internal decoration. When the containers are standing side by side each gecko should not have eye contact with its neighbour. The furnishings should be as simple as possible, making the container easy to clean. For many species a loosely crumpled sheet of kitchen tissue is quite suitable as a substrate. If this is thought to be too spartan then the base may be covered by a shallow layer of sand or potting compost. A short but sturdy branch and a small climbing plant—e.g., *Ficus pumila*—should also be installed. For ground-dwelling species or those from arid desert regions, the plant is not neccessary and should be replaced by a few pieces of bark, cork, or natural rock under which the young may hide.

Whilst very little light is required for rearing nocturnal geckoes, and only the temperature is of any importance, day geckoes require light and heat in large measure. If large numbers of day geckoes are being reared regularly it is expedient to construct a special rearing

Above: Phelsuma standingi hatching.
Below: Rhacodactylus auriculatus hatching.

Newly-hatched Geckolepis.

cabinet in the form of a set of drawers. Above each drawer containing the rearing containers there should be several fluorescent tubes and small halogen lights. Both should be fitted with good reflectors and should be as close as possible to the top of the rearing containers. The heat thus generated is enormous, and must be dispersed by a ventilator connected to an electronic thermostat. For some species excellent lighting is decisive for the development of the typical adult colouring. Young which are reared under insufficient light will frequently not have the colour intensity of young which grow up in the wild, (although this condition can have other causes).

The young must be serviced daily. The rearing container should be lightly sprayed and fresh food in the form of Drosophila or small crickets introduced. The food should always be dusted with a good vitamin/mineral preparation. The size of the rearing containers should increase with the size of the animals but should never be too large. This can prevent the young from catching their food insects, leading to gradual starvation.

FEEDING

Not only correct husbandry is vital when keeping geckoes. A balanced and adequate diet must also be guaranteed. Nowadays the quantities of food required present no problems. It can be bought in pet shops or ordered directly from the supplier in any quantity. Nevertheless, the selection is quite restricted and very rarely are more than ten different foods available. It is therefore important that, when feeding the animals, certain vitamins, minerals, and amino acids be added to bring the food to the required quality.

Feeding geckoes is really quite easy because they will eat almost anything of a suitable size. In the wild their food consists mainly of insects, spiders, and small vertebrates which they seize very quickly. As well as this animal matter, a large number of species will also eat fruit and flower nectar. Some species have an enormous food range. *Gekko gecko*, for example, will eat small snakes, nestling mice, and birds. In general it can be said that not all gecko species will eat nestling mice. Unfortunately, many will eat other lizards, including their own young. Eggs too are a welcome alternative, irrespective of whether they are the animals' own or those of another species. Some voracious species will even attempt to eat something which is much too large for them and choke in the process. There are also some feeding specialists amongst the geckoes. *Rhynchoedura ornata*, a species from the Australian desert, eats only ants and termites. Such species are therefore not suitable for keeping in captivity.

Earlier not enough attention was given to the fruit portion of the diet of geckoes. For instance the New Caledonian Giant Geckoes of the genus *Rhacodactylus* eat a large amount of fruit. Some animals regularly take large bites of fruit. It is a very interesting sight to see *Rhacodactylus leachianus* eating a banana. Whilst kept in a vivarium or during transport, many species such as *Phelsuma* may be fed on fruit.

Ailuronyx lapping baby food.

The question of who eats fruit and who does not is difficult to answer. It is well-known that ground dwellers do not eat fruit and for some of the tree dwellers this is also true. There is no alternative than to try feeding the hatchlings on fruit.

Our geckoes are fed on a great variety of foods such as springtails, large and small Drosophila, corn and waxmoths and their larvae, mealworms, Zophobas, house crickets, field crickets, various species of beetles, and nestling mice. Some geckoes enjoy bananas, papayas, and other sweet fruit, as well as ready-made fruit compotes normally used for young children. They appear to prefer a variety which contains banana. The fruit compote also has the advantage that it already contains added vitamins and minerals. Unfortunately, some geckoes also have a distinct preference for a certain type of food animal. This may only be avoided by offering a wide variety of food so that a preference may not develop.

Some species, usually those from regions in which there is not a great deal of variation in the food on offer, often tend toward obesity when kept in captivity. A regular check should be made of whether the animals eat and what they eat. It is not only these species which tend toward obesity. Others show the same tendency because in the vivarium they are not as active as they would be in the wild. Usually they do not have to search for long periods to find food or to find a mate, nor do they have to defend a territory from rivals or flee from enemies. The geckoes should therefore be encouraged to become more active. Instead of feeding 3 large crickets, give the animals 30 small insects. The geckoes will usually enjoy these more.

The time at which food is given should be the same as that at which the animals would feed in the wild, and this can vary from species to species. Thus nocturnal geckoes should be fed in the late evening so that the food insects cannot hide or shake off the vitamin/mineral powder with which they have been coated. According to the origin of its occupants, the vivarium should be sprayed up to three times each day giving the geckoes an opportunity to drink. It is vital that each vivarium also contains a small shallow water bowl which enables the geckoes to drink at any time.

BREEDING FOOD INSECTS

Nowadays, the most diverse types of insects may be obtained from pet shops, or by ordering direct from the supplier. Nevertheless, it is advisable when time and space permit to also breed one's own supplies of food. The advantages are obvious; as well as being independent of any shortage of supply which the dealer may experience, or any losses during transport, there is the guarantee that high quality nourishing insects are always available. It is only if the insects are fed a high-value and varied diet that the necessary quality will be achieved. Mention should also be made of the disadvantages of breeding one's own insects. These are the time involved as well as the noise and smells which are present even in the most well-ordered breeding establishment. In the following we give a short description of the most important insect breeding methods. Further details may be found in the book by Friedrich & Volland (1981) which we highly recommend.

Short Descriptions of Some Insect Breeding Methods

Small and large wingless Drosophila

Container: Glass jars, 0.5 l volume.
Temperature: 25 °C

Breeding:	Cook 500 g wholemeal rolled oats to a thick paste. Add a pinch of Nipagin™, a packet of dried yeast, and two tablespoons of grape sugar. Stir well. When the paste has cooled place it into the jars to a depth of 4 cm. Place a roughly crumpled piece of kitchen tissue on the paste and introduce the breeding colony of around 50 fruit flies. Seal the jar with a piece of cotton or muslin and a rubber band. The development of the small variety requires 2 weeks, that of the large variety 4 weeks. Before being fed to geckoes the Drosophila should be liberally coated with a powdered vitamin/mineral preparation.

Large and small waxmoths

Container:	Use only metal containers covered by very fine gauze. Soft plastic will be eaten by the caterpillars.
Temperature:	28 °C.
Breeding:	Fill the container with old honeycomb or artificial food which may easily be made from the recipe provided by Friedrich & Volland (1981). Place around 20 moths in the container, which should be kept warm. The development of a new generation takes 6–7 weeks. Before removing the moths, stand the container in a cool place for a short time. If caterpillars are required these must be sought amongst the moths' food.

Field crickets and house crickets

Container:	A high-sided plastic aquarium or similar container with a tightly fitting cover.
Temperature:	28 °C.
Breeding:	Several egg cartons and a suitable place for the crickets to lay their eggs should be placed on the bottom of the aquarium. A suitable container for egg-laying is a 5 cm high plastic container filled with a sand/peat mixture which is kept constantly moist. So that the crickets do not immediately eat the newly laid eggs the

container should be covered by fine fly gauze. The crickets should be fed on dog flakes or pellets. Carrots and fruit should be given as moist food. A drinking bowl should always be available. A suitable drinking system is a bird drinker, the opening of which is loosely packed with cotton wool. Development from egg to adult takes 8–10 weeks for field crickets and 7–10 weeks for house crickets. It is sufficient to check the breeding container at 3-day intervals, adding food if necessary. The crickets can be removed by shaking the egg cartons into a high-sided plastic container.

Large black beetles (Zophobas)

Container:
For the adults a plastic aquarium with tightly fitting cover. For the larvae an open, high-sided container is sufficient.

Temperature:
28 °C.

Breeding:
The container should be filled to a depth of 5 cm with wood shavings upon which large pieces of bark should be placed. The beetles will lay their eggs in the cracks and crevices in the bark. The larvae hatch after 8–12 days. For proper development the eggs require a certain amount of moisture; therefore the container should be lightly sprayed daily. Every 14 days the beetles should be collected from the container and the larvae removed to a separate container. Replace the wood shavings, bark, and beetles to recommence the process. This procedure should be repeated every 14 days so that larvae of all sizes are constantly available. At around 8 weeks the larvae have reached their full size. To allow some of the larvae to metamorphose into insects they should be placed in individual glass jars where they may pupate and turn eventually into adult beetles. Those are then placed with the other adults in the main container. The beetles may be fed

on dry cat or dog food in pellet form. Carrots, potatoes, green food, and fruit should be given to provide moisture. Only the larvae should be fed to geckoes.

Argentinian cockroaches

Container:	A plastic aquarium with tightly fitting cover.
Temperature:	28 °C.
Breeding:	Place an egg carton on a 2 cm layer of dog flakes. Fresh moist food should be given twice each week. The most suitable moist food is carrot. Development takes a long time; from young to adult around six months. They should therefore only be fed to the geckoes when it is obvious that they are reproducing well and regularly.

VITAMINS, MINERALS, AND AMINO ACIDS

This is one of the most important subjects, upon which there are as many opinions as there are herpetologists. One thing is certain; irrespective of how good and varied the diet is in captivity, it is never as nourishing or as beneficial as that found in the wild. For this reason the food given in captivity should always be enriched.

Without doubt the best food for geckoes in captivity is meadow sweepings, i.e., insects caught by sweeping a large net through the vegetation. This however we do not use because of the dangers from herbicides and pesticides, as wall as for the protection of wildlife. The minimum dietary supplements which should be given to geckoes are calcium and vitamin D_3, because insects from artificial breeding centres inevitably have an imbalance of calcium and phosphates.

Any preparation containing only calcium and vitamin D_3 is suitable for geckoes, allowing them to reproduce without any illnesses caused by deficiencies. Many geckoes will willingly eat the calcium provided by finely powdered cuttlefish bone. This is especially important for gravid females. Some species eat the remains of the shells after the young have hatched.

DISEASES AND TREATMENT

Since like many other herpetologists we are frequently asked about diagnoses and treatment, we wish to give some information on those illnesses which are easy to recognise and their treatment. We consider it best to avoid illnesses and keep the geckoes healthy by correct husbandry. Nevertheless, despite the best husbandry, illnesses do occasionally occur. So as not to be totally helpless in such situations, we advise that the following literature be obtained well in advance.

First and foremost the book by Isenbügel & Frank (1985), because the medications mentioned in this publication are generally available. We also recommend the German book by Ippen & Else (1985), and the excellent and comprehensive book in English by Cooper & Jackson (1981).

We strongly advise visiting only those veterinary surgeons who have considerable experience with reptiles. This will save both time and unnecessary expense.

In every case a wild-caught animal or one from an unknown source should be placed in isolation for some weeks. To do this the animal should be placed in a simple container which is easy to clean and which is very sparsely furnished. After being placed in the quarantine container the gecko should be fed and watered. The first excrement produced should be sent to a laboratory with the request that it be examined microscopically for illnesses or parasites and that advice be given regarding any necessary treatment. If the excrement shows no evidence of parasites a further sample should be sent after 3 weeks. If this too is negative, the animal may be placed in the vivarium which is to house it. If parasites are found the animal should be treated as advised and a further excrement sample sent to the laboratory after several days. If during the quarantine period the animal should die from an unknown cause, the remains may also be sent to the laboratory for autopsy. The most common illnesses and possible treatments are described below.

Sloughing Problems

Sloughing problems usually occur because of simple husbandry errors such as geckoes being kept under conditions which are either too moist or too dry. Whilst sloughing some animals do not enjoy being sprayed. Because some animals will not shed the entire skin in one day, the husbandry conditions should be varied slightly, and a few days allowed to elapse, before the remainder of the skin is removed manually. If, however, negative signs occur, such as swellings on the unsloughed parts of the body, action must be taken immediately. The animals should be either bathed in lukewarm water containing camomile lotion, or an unperfumed cream should be massaged into the old skin, after which the old skin should be gently and carefully removed. With young geckoes this is a very arduous process which, if it is to be prolonged, should be interrupted at intervals to prevent distressing the animal.

Rachitis

This is a very wide-ranging term. It means all illnesses caused by deficiency of vitamins, especially vitamin D_3 or a deficiency of minerals, as well as a deficiency of certain amino acids. This illness cannot be fully described and only some of the symptoms are described here. These are, for example, soft bones which are easily felt around the jaws, curvature of the spine and the tail, short limbs, and shortened jaws. These symptoms usually appear during adolescence or in females during the breeding season, and they can be avoided by providing adequate vitamins, minerals, and amino acids. If signs of the illness are already visible a multi-vitamin product should be added to the drinking water. In addition 0.01 to 1 drop of Multimulsin™, depending upon size should be given to the animal orally each week. Geckoes which regularly eat small mammals will rarely suffer from vitamin or mineral deficiencies.

Mites

Mites are external parasites which are easily visible and which live on the blood of their host. Newly obtained animals should be carefully examined for the presence of mites which, if detected, should be treated immediately. If not, they will not only continue to weaken their host, but may spread disease. The infected animal should be placed in a cotton bag which has been soaked in a 0.2% solution of Neguvon™ and then dried. The animal should remain in this bag for 1 hour. If the mites have been carried into the vivarium, all other animals must be treated individually and placed temporarily in another container. A Vapona™ strip should be suspended in the vivarium for one week and the ventilation panels sealed. After 1 week the vivarium should be thoroughly ventilated before the geckoes are reintroduced.

Injuries

If a gecko has sustained a wound which is not yet infected it may be bathed with gentian violet—5% gentian violet in 70% alcohol. Ask a chemist to mix this solution. If the wounds are infected only an antibiotic cream will help.

Egg Binding

Females frequently suffer from this condition, which is almost invariably caused by incorrect husbandry, e.g., no suitable place to lay their eggs or inadequate feeding. If a female is egg bound only an injection of Oxytocin™ will help. This should be administered at a dosage of around 30 ml per kg of body weight and should be injected into the first one-third of the tail. Very divergent results have been obtained with Oxytocin. If Oxytocin fails the eggs will remain in the body of the female and eventually cause death. If an antibiotic is needed to treat inflamations such as mouth rot, Baytril™ should be given orally at a dosage of 40 mg per kg of body weight. Great success has been achieved with this medication.

Vivarium Technology

In this day and age herpetology without technical aids is totally un-thinkable. In a fully automated vivarium they reduce the daily workload to feeding and cleaning. They also give the keeper the inde-pendence to spend a few days away from home without the problem of needing someone to look in on the animals every day, and they allow more time simply to observe the animals.

TIME SWITCH

The time switch operates the lighting, heating, and, if installed, the spraying or misting units by switching them on and off at predeter-mined times. By using a time switch the regularity of day and night is achieved, this being very beneficial for the animals. In addition the time switch also permits the seasons and other periodic variations to be closely approximated. For example, it is easy to determine by ex-perimentation when and for how long the heating should be switched on so that the temperature does not drop too dramatically and that the vivarium remains warm enough, but does not get too hot for its occu-pants. If these conditions had to be governed manually it would in it-self be a full day's work. Various types of time switch are available commercially, but we strongly recommend the recently introduced digital time switches, which like their mechanical counterparts, need only to be plugged in. They provide a very short switching time (the shortest is around one minute) and a very long-lasting effect. In addi-tion, they may be programmed optionally for weekly or monthly op-eration.

HEATING

The vivarium heating system is one of the most important pieces of equipment because the temperature is the most important factor for natural daily activity. Whilst the natural activity of day geckoes is regulated somewhat by the light intensity, the natural activity of nocturnal geckoes is governed solely by the temperature. This means that in the vivarium the temperature must always remain within the natural activity range for each species being kept. Even if the temperature of the room is within the range of most gecko species, some warmer spots must be provided, enabling the geckoes to reach the temperature which they prefer.

A day-night variation is also vital, enabling rest and activity periods to be recognised. For many species an annual cycle of temperature variations is also vital as a trigger for reproduction.

The method of heating is different for diurnal and nocturnal geckoes. For species which are active during the day the most natural form of heating is provided by heating from above using reflector lamps or spotlights. Here various options are available. If the vivarium is illuminated by a HQL or HQI lamp, this usually also provides adequate heating. Normal spotlights or low voltage halogen lamps with reflectors are also suitable. One disadvantage here is that the plants which grow near the lamps are easily burned. For this reason all radiant heat sources should be directed on to a "basking place", e.g. onto rocks.

For nocturnal geckoes radiant heat has almost no significance. It is true that some species occasionally bask but this is usually when they are unable to reach their preferred temperature in any other way. Because when using radiant heat a great deal of energy is "wasted" on producing light which is no use to some species, it is better to use a different heating system.

There are many other ways to heat a vivarium. The first are inductance coils of fluorescent lighting and metal vapour discharge lamps. These should be installed below the vivarium. Other means of heating which are widely available are heat pads, heating foil, and heating cable. Using any of these heating media, the vivarium should be only partially heated and never above 35 °C, so that the geckoes have retiring places with lower temperatures. If a heating cable or heating pad is to be used in the vivarium, it should be placed in position before the furnishings are installed. To prevent its being excavated by the vivarium occupants it should be fixed in position using silicon sealer. It is almost impossible to install a heating cable below the substrate afterwards. When one end has been carefully concealed, the next piece usually pulls it out again. The heating cable must never lie on the surface of the substrate. Crickets will chew through its protective outer casing, making it no longer waterproof. Heating foil should always be installed below the vivarium.

Before the geckoes are installed in the vivarium, the temperatures should be carefully measured using a maximum/minimum thermometer in various positions. This will indicate whether the heating equipment is functioning in the way it has been preset. When the animals are in the vivarium, a thermometer and a hair-hygrometer should also be present, enabling defects to be immediately detected. In rain forest vivaria the heating equipment must always be installed below the substrate to maintain high relative atmospheric humidity.

Various problems can arise with the vivarium heating equipment. For example, how to prevent overheating. To solve this problem use should be made of one of the many electronically controlled thermostats, which are now readily available commercially. These come with a measurement feeler and several metres of cable, which can be easily concealed inside the vivarium whilst the thermostat mechanism itself remains outside the vivarium. The electrical current for the heating equipment and the time switch must be controlled by this thermostat. Thus, when a certain temperature is reached, the heating is automatically switched off. Anyone attaching great value to additional safety should install a second electronically controlled thermostat which, when an even higher temperature is reached, will switch on a ventilator to cool the vivarium.

In practice it has proved expedient to connect such an electronic thermostat to the room heating and lighting (this too produces a great deal of heat). When a certain temperature is reached the thermostat will switch off all heating and lighting, switching them on again when the temperature drops below the lowest preset limit. With an electronically controlled thermostat there is also the possibility of controlling only the heating. When buying the thermostat care should be taken that a device which allows a nightly reduction is purchased.

When keeping species from the temperate regions a calendar should also be available. This should record the entire annual sequence of day length and length of heating period. The clocks on the time switches should be set according to this calendar.

LIGHTING

Because of the different activity periods of diurnal and nocturnal geckoes, the lighting system also serves two completely different basic functions.

In the case of nocturnal geckoes the lighting plays only a subsidiary role. It is basically for the benefit of any plants in the vivarium, and to imitate the day/night rhythm. If no plants are present a single fluorescent tube is quite adequate. A vivarium for nocturnal geckoes should be illuminated for 12 hours each day. It is only for species from the temperate regions that the day length (period of illumination) should vary.

Lighting for diurnal geckoes is of enormous importance. As well as the basic provision of day and night and annual cycle, their entire activity depends to a great extent on high light intensity. In the tropics the light intensity in the sun is around 1,000,000 Lux, whilst in the shade of a tree it is still around 10,000 Lux. In comparison, the light intensity on a covered balcony is only 500 Lux and behind a window around 2,000 Lux. From these figures it can be seen that the light intensity provided in a vivarium can only closely approximate the values provided in the wild. For this reason, and to conserve energy, only high value fluorescent tubes (e.g., LUMILUX DE LUXE by Osram) should be used. By using a good reflector the light intensity can be increased by a further 40%.

To give day geckoes even further possibilities of greater light intensity and slightly increased warmth, the vivarium should also have at least one low-voltage halogen lamp with a small angle of radiation of 10–15°. In this spotlight day geckoes will often "top-up" on light and heat.

The usual incandescent lamps and spotlights are normally used only for heating because the light intensity they produce is too low. The light intensity of a 40 W incandescent lamp at a distance of one metre is only 35 lux.

In the selection of the colours of light from fluorescent tubes, a combination of the colors "daylight" and "warmtone" has proved the most comfortable and normal for human eyes. The colour of the light appears to be unimportant for geckoes, but the most suitable would be "daylight" because this closely resembles the spectrum of the sun.

An important question is: How many tubes should be fitted above each vivarium? This question can not be answered simply, because the requirements of the individual species and the plants are different. Experimentation will show when the animals become most active and show their most beautiful colours. Unfortunately, to date there have been no in-depth investigations into the light intensity at which geckoes carry out certain behavioural patterns. One thing is certain: When the light intensity is too low, certain species will not reproduce. Some species which require very high light intensity are *Phelsuma serraticauda* and *Lygodactylus picturatus*.

Vivaria up to a height of 80 cm can be adequately illuminated by fluorescent tubes. Taller vivaria should only be illuminated by special HQL and HQI lamps. In addition to normal vivarium lighting, there are many other special lamps which may be used, such as metal vapour discharge lamps. Of these lamps, the HQI lamps are especially recommended since their colour spectrum closely resembles that of sunlight, and they provide the greatest amount of light. They may be bought in strengths from 35 W. Unfortunately, they are very expensive to buy, but in comparison with other lamps and the amount of energy they consume, HQI lamps are quite economic to use.

For diurnal geckoes the lights should be on for 12–14 hours each day. If the vivarium stands in a room which is used regularly, the geckoes will quickly become accustomed to the movements outside and will not be disturbed by them. The geckoes may then be observed without encroaching upon them in any way.

UV LIGHT IN THE VIVARIUM?

A recurring question is: Do the animals require ultraviolet light ? In our experience this question may be answered with a simple "No", provided the animals are given sufficient vitamin D_3. This reply does not disregard the vitamin D_3 synthesis obtained from UV radiation, but the geckoes are better able to meet their vitamin D_3 requirements from the artificial food. The problem is considered in more detail below.

To date there is no exact indication of what percentage of the UV radiation penetrates the skin, thus triggering the vitamin D synthesis. There is no argument that in the light range of 315 to 350 nm the vitamin D synthesis is active in the body of the animals. Nevertheless, investigations of the penetration of the skin have given divergent results. Nietzke (1990) writes that the penetration of UV rays 225 to 350 nm lies between 35 and 68% tested on various pieces of skin from reptile sloughs. Molle, Dohrn & Lehmann (1961) measured on a live *Phelsuma Lineata* a penetration of only 0.1%. Compared with human skin (penetration around 30%) this is very low.

Anyone wishing to be certain to provide the geckoes with UV radiation should use fluorescent tubes with the "daylight" colour or metal vapour discharge lamps because both have a certain UV proportion.

It should be remembered that glass filters UV light completely. The UV lights should therefore be fitted above gauze or Perspex™.

Strong UV lamps such as Ultravitalux are not recommended because the reptiles show no signs of exposure (as does human skin by turning red), when the critical amount of radiation has been reached.

For nocturnal geckoes these questions are superfluous since their activity time in the wild only begins after sundown.

SPRAYING AND MISTING UNITS

If there are only one or two vivaria the spraying can be carried out daily by hand. What happens, however, during holidays, or if several vivaria are to be serviced, or simply if more time is desired to observe the animals? In such cases it is expedient to fit a completely automated spraying installation.

By fitting such an installation, the animals can be regularly sprayed, which is very advantageous for them. It also provides the keeper with the great advantage of independence, enabling him to leave even rain forest species for several days without having someone to care for the animals daily.

There is now commercially available a spraying unit which has become increasingly popular and which can be built from individual components. In a rented apartment the spraying unit operates by means of a high pressure pump, normally marketed as a high pressure cleaner, but in a private house it can also be operated by the normal pressure in the water pipes. A water pipe should be installed to the vivaria, and a magnet valve attached to the end. A magnet valve may be obtained from a discarded washing machine or purchased from an electrical retailer. The magnet valve or the pump are controlled by a digital time switch. If the shortest switching time (around 1 minute) is still too long, e.g, for desert vivaria, a domestic lighting relay may be connected to the time switch. By this means, switching times shorter than 1 minute can be achieved. Using a rubber tube system, the nozzles are installed in the vivarium and connected to the magnet valve or pump.

There are then two possibilities: Spray only as much water as will evaporate or be absorbed by the plants, as in a desert vivarium, or install a drainage system. This requires a hole in the base of the vivarium into which a tight-fitting drainage pipe is inserted and subsequently sealed. This allows excess water to drain into a container placed below the vivarium. It is important that the drain cover is surrounded by a filter material which prevents solid matter from entering the drainage pipe.

When using a spraying system which is connected directly to the water system, a fine filter should be fitted in front of the magnet valve. This guarantees more efficient operation of the unit and prevents minute particles from entering the magnet valve to stop it closing properly. Even greater safety is achieved by fitting two magnet valves, one behind the other, in case one should fail to close. As a safeguard against the final weak point—the time switch—a domestic lighting relay should be installed in the switching circuit. This interrupts the current as soon as the set time has been reached and thus prevents the unit from spraying longer than intended.

It is only recently that ultrasound humidifiers have been used as misting units for herpetological purposes, i.e., to create the effect of rain in vivaria. These misting units more often provide an optical show than they meet the drinking requirements of the geckoes. It is very interesting to see the vivarium slowly fill with mist which takes some time to condense before the vivarium is once again clear. To guarantee that sufficient water remains in the vivarium, and that sufficient mist turns to "dew" rather than evaporates, the ultrasound air humidifier must also be in operation for some time. This type of "rain" is very beneficial for species from the Namib Desert where each evening a mist comes in from the sea and condenses. With this type of moisturisation the conditions prevalent there are closely approximated.

The main task is to maintain the relative air humidity in the vivaria. Therefore the plants must be watered and additional spraying must be carried out. When a misting unit is used to humidify a vivarium, careful tests should be carried out to determine how long the unit should be in operation before additional spraying and watering are no longer required.

If geckoes are kept together with frogs a misting unit is absolutely essential, because as soon as misting commences the frogs become more active.

For a misting unit, an air humidifier is required. These are readily available as are humidifiers which are modified for use in vivaria. Before purchase a check should be made to ensure that the device has a built-in decalcifier. Again the misting unit must be controlled by a time switch. A system of pipes should be attached at the outlet of the ultrasound air humidifier. The pipes must be installed in such a way that water which condenses in them flows back to the humidifier or drips into the vivarium. The pipes to the vivarium should be 7 cm in diameter whilst those in the individual vivaria should be around 3.5 cm. The open ends of the pipes in the vivaria should be covered with gauze to prevent geckoes entering. The ventilation panels should be also covered with fine gauze.

With a high-powered unit, 4–10 medium-sized vivaria may be simultaneously misted.

Geckoes Frequently Kept in Captivity

In the following, descriptions are given of all subfamilies of the Geckonidae as well as all important data regarding appearance, husbandry, and reproduction. A rough survey of the distribution ranges and genera can be found on page 4. The various types of vivaria are designated I to V. More information on these can be found on pages 65–69. The letter-key used in the survey of the subfamilies gives information regarding the exact habitats of the individual genera:

A = Ground dweller, B = Tree dweller, C = Bush dweller, D = Cliff dweller

SUBFAMILY EUBLEPHARINAE
(LIDDED GECKOES)

Genera	Species	Distribution	Vivarium	Habitat
Aeluroscalabotes	2	1c, 2?	IV	A
Coleonyx	8	4a, 5	I, II, or IV	A
Eublepharis	4	1	I	A
Goniurosaurus	2	1	III	A
Hemitheconyx	2	3b	III	A
Holodactylus	2	3b	I	A

The subfamily Eublepharinae, nowadays usually regarded as a separate family, is the oldest and most original of all geckoes. The name Lidded Geckoes is appropriate and refers to the main characteristic of moveable eyelids. The eyes are closed whilst sleeping. To achieve this the eyelids are moved upwards. The pupil is vertical and in a bright light is reduced to a very narrow slit. None of these genera managed to develop clinging lamellae and for this reason they are predominantly ground dwellers. They reproduce by laying two soft-shelled eggs which are buried in the substrate. All species are entirely nocturnal.

Coleonyx (Gray, 1845)

The eight species of this genus live in the south of North America to Central America, whilst *C. elegans* is distributed from southern Mexico to Central America and lives in a moist habitat. *C. variegatus* can be found from northern Mexico to North America and lives in deserts and semi-deserts. These two species and their subspecies cover an enormous range and all of these animals are terrestrial.

Coleonyx variegatus (Baird, 1859)

Distribution: Southwestern United States, northeastern Mexico
Habitat: Dry, stony semi-desert and desert regions. Lives beneath rocks and in rocky hollows.
Size: Up to 140 mm.
Characteristics: Moveable eyelid. The toes end in a nonretractile claw. The feet do not have any clinging mechanism. The ground colour is yellow and the upper body and tail are covered with brown transverse bands. These are partially interrupted by darker brown spots. The underside of the body is white without any pigmentation. Instead of transverse bands, regenerated tails have only irregular brown spots. Because of the significant sexual dimorphism the sexes are easily distinguished. On each side of the root of the tail the males have a spur around 1 mm long. In females this is very minute or absent. The males also have well-developed hemipenes pockets.
Vivarium: Types I and III. A suitable substrate is fine sand. Rocks should be arranged to form small caves which serve as hiding places.
Husbandry and reproduction: Daylight hours are spent beneath rocks or in the caves. A vivarium with a ground area of 0.2 m² is quite adequate for a group of 3–4 animals. Because the animals rarely climb, the height of the vivarium is of no great importance. Two males cannot be housed together; only several females will tolerate one another. During copulation the male bites the female on the neck. The eggs are laid

Coleonyx variegatus.

between April and October. There are always two soft-shelled eggs which grow significantly during incubation. Shortly before the hatching of the 55–58 mm young, the eggs reach a size of 19 mm long and 9 mm wide. At a temperature of 28 °C (± 1 °C) the eggs take 52–56 days to hatch and with good feeding the young may reach sexual maturity in 1 year. A cool period of 4–6 weeks at temperatures of 10–15 °C stimulates mating.

Food: Crickets, small locusts, springtails, mealworms, waxmoth larvae.
Similar species: *C. brevis* as well as all subspecies of *C. variegatus, C. switaki, C. reticulatus.*

Eublepharis (Gray, 1827)

Although *E. macularius* is one of the geckoes most frequently kept in vivaria, the other species are almost unknown. *E. angramainyu* grows to around 25 cm and lives in the region of the Zagros Mountains in Iran. *E. turcmenicus* was only introduced to science by Darevsky in

Eublepharis macularius.

1977. This species lives in Turkmenistan. All species live on the ground in dry to semi-dry areas.

Eublepharis macularius (Blyth, 1854)

Distribution: Afghanistan, Iraq, Iran, northwest India.
Habitat: Dry to semi-dry desert regions. During daylight hours these animals hide beneath rocks or in holes in the ground.
Size: 220 mm.
Characteristics: The common name, Leopard Gecko, is very appropriate. The ground colour is yellow with irregular black spots. The original tail is segmented. The feet do not have any clinging lamellae and the toes end in a small claw. Because of the moveable eyelids these animals can close their eyes. The underside of the body is white. In gravid females the eggs can be clearly seen through the skin.
Vivarium: Type I. The ground area for a group of 1–3 animals must not be less than 0.2 m². The animals should be able to hide beneath rocks or pieces of bark.

Juvenile Eublepharis macularius.

Husbandry and reproduction: *Eublepharis macularius* is one of the most frequently bred species of gecko. It is advisable to keep a group of one male and two or more females. Two males kept together will not tolerate one another. Males are easily recognised by their preanal pores. A short reduction of the temperature from 25 °C to 15 °C for 4 weeks has a stimulating effect on mating. The eggs, which measure around 28 × 15 mm, are buried in the substrate. For this reason part of the vivarium should always be kept moist. A potted plant placed in the vivarium will often be chosen for egg laying. The eggs should be transferred to an incubator because the adult geckoes will eat the young. The young, which are around 85 mm long, hatch after 45–53 days at a temperature of 28 °C. They have a wonderfully contrasting pattern and have one of the most beautiful juvenile colourings amongst all nocturnal geckoes. Rearing the young presents no problems.

Food: Crickets, small locusts, waxmoth larvae, mealworms, springtails, grasshoppers, and nestling mice.

Similar species: *E. angramainyu, E. hardwicki, E. turcmenicus,* and all subspecies of *E. macularius.*

Goniurosaurus kuriowae splendens.

Goniurosaurus (Barbour, 1908)

It had long been expected that the species *E. kuroiwae* and *E. lichten-felderi* would be reclassified into a separate genus. Whilst the species *G. kuroiwae* and the subspecies *G. k. orientalis* and *G. k. splendens* are described from the Ryukyu Islands, the species *G. lichtenfelderi* occurs on the Norway Islands and Hainan Island in the Gulf of Tonkin. They are terrestrial and belong to the group of Lidded Geckoes.

Goniurosaurus kuroiwae splendens (Nakumura & Ueno, 1959)

Distribution: Ryukyu Islands of Japan.
Habitat: These are clawed geckoes which live amongst limestone rocks. During daylight hours they hide in holes where there is always a higher ambient humidity.
Size: 160 mm.
Characteristics: These geckoes have a slender body and a very pointed head. The ground colour is a blackish-brown. Across the back there are four reddish-pink transverse bands which start at the neck and end at

the root of the tail. Between the bands there are some irregular reddish-pink spots. The blackish-brown tail is interspaced by several white
transverse bands. The males can easily be distinguished by their well-
developed hemipenes pockets. *G. k. splendens* is the only species which
is banded.

Vivarium: Type III. Several pieces of cork bark should be available
as hiding places. An area of substrate should always be kept moist.
Because these geckoes frequently climb, several branches should be
placed in the vivarium. The temperature should range between 18 and
30 °C, but no higher. Several potted plants complete the vivarium furnishings.

Husbandry and reproduction: Males will not tolerate one another. In
a roomy vivarium several females may be kept with one male. These
animals show their anger by waving the tail. Approximately every 4
weeks the females lay two soft-shelled eggs in one of their hiding
places (beneath cork bark). They lay around three clutches each year.
The females guard the eggs for 2 days. Shortly before hatching the eggs
reach a size of 20 × 12 mm. At a temperature of 27 °C the young hatch
after 65–70 days and measure 55–60 mm. They require high humidity
for their development. The young should be fed on small waxmoth larvae, wingless fruitfly, small crickets, and locusts.

Food: Waxmoth larvae, small locusts, crickets.

Hemitheconyx (Stejneger, 1893)

To date two species of this genus have been described. Whilst the species *H. caudicinctus* occurs in West Africa, *H. taylori* lives in Somalia
in East Africa. Both species are terrestrial.

Hemitheconyx caudicinctus (A. Duméril, 1851)

Distribution: West Africa from Senegal to Cameroon.

Habitat: These animals live on the open savannah and also in forest
areas. Long constantly dry periods are often as common as rains last-
ing for weeks.

Size: 200 mm.

Characteristics: An elongated, cylindrical ground-dwelling gecko with
very short legs. The toes end in a short claw. The original tail is segmented. Regenerated tails appear to be common and are fat and bul-

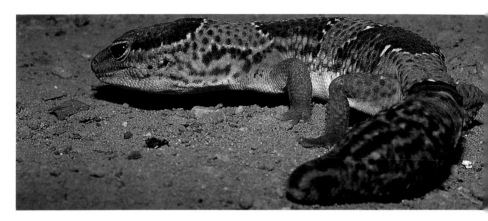

Hemitheconyx caudicinctus.

bous. The colouring consists of various tones of brown. There are two darker brown transverse bands across the back. In addition the tail and top of the head down to the snout are the same dark brown. Between the transverse bands the colouring can be reddish-brown to yellow. A white stripe from the centre of the head to the tail has only been seen in a few individual specimens. The underside is white without any markings.

Vivarium: Type III. The height of the vivarium is not important, but a large floor area is essential. Hiding places made from stacked flat rocks or pieces of tree bark will immediately be utilised. Moist places are preferred.

Husbandry and reproduction: These animals must not be kept under conditions which are too dry. They have been bred quite frequently, but incubating the eggs usually causes problems. The eggs are always buried in moist substrate so it would appear that they need to be incubated under more moist conditions than other soft-shelled eggs. The young, which hatch with a length of around 70 mm, can be reared without difficulty. One male can be kept with several females, but males will not tolerate one another. They can be easily distinguished by their well-developed preanal pores.

Food: Crickets, small locusts, grasshoppers, waxmoth larvae, mealworms, springtails, pink mice.

SUBFAMILY DIPLODACTYLINAE
(DOUBLE-FINGERED GECKOES)

Genera	Species	Distribution	Vivarium	Habitat
Bavayia	5	9	IV	B
Carphodactylus	1	2	IV	B
Crenadactylus	1	3	II	B
Diplodactylus	36	2	I, II, III	A, C
Eurodactylodes	2	9	IV	C
Heteropholis*	6	8	III	C
Hoplodactylus	10	8	III	B
Naultinus*	2	8	III	C
Nephrurus	7	8	I	A
Oedura	13	2	III, IV	B, D
Phyllurus	4	2	IV, V	B, D
Pseudothecadactylus	2	2	IV, V	B, D
Rhacdactylus	6	9	III	B
Rhynchoedura	1	2	I	A
Underwoodisaurus	2	2	III	A

* Diurnal genera

The subfamily Diplodactylinae is limited to Australia, New Zealand, New Caledonia, and the Loyalty Islands. This subfamily is distinguished by the fact that the females of all species lay soft-shelled eggs, whilst the genera *Heteropholis, Hoplodactylus, Naultinus*, and *Rhacodactylus trachyrhynchus* give birth to live young. With the exception of *R. chahoua* there are no cases of double-eggs because soft-shelled eggs do not stick together.

Bavayia (Roux, 1913)

The subspecies *B. cyclura montana* and *B. cyclura crassicollis* were only elevated to species status by A. Bauer in 1989. The species described in 1869 by Bavay as *Platydactylus crepuscularis* and later as *Hemiphyllodactylus typus typus* was reclassified in 1989 by Ross A. Sadlier as *Bavayia septuiclavis* and a second species as *Bavayia validiclavis*. In the

Bavayia montana.

process he would certainly have been tempted to arrange the two species in a new genus.

To date all species have not yet been described. Here, mention
should be made of a new species which distinguishes itself considerably from the others by its size: *Bavayia spec*. It has a total length of
over 20 cm. The species *B. montana, B. cyclura*, and *B. crassicollis* live
on trees, whilst the species *B. sauvagei, B. septuiclavis*, and *B. validiclavis* spend the day on the ground amongst rotting wood and only
climb into the bushes at night.

B. sauvagei is distinguished from the other species in that the claws
on the little fingers are not in the centre.

Bavayia montana (Roux, 1913)

Distribution: New Caledonia.
Habitat: The day is spent beneath loose tree bark or amongst the root systems of tree ferns. They are inhabitants of the rain forests and lead a purely arboreal lifestyle.
Size: 140 mm.
Characteristics: The ground colour is a brownish-yellow with a dark brown pigmentation. There are irregular light spots scattered over the body. As opposed to *B. cyclura, B. montana* does not have any neck bands. There are no markings on the underside.
Vivarium: Type IV. The vivarium must be higher than it is wide and should not be less than 50 cm tall. The furnishings consist of several climbing branches and vertical cork tubes as hiding places.
Husbandry and reproduction: The husbandry is the same as that described for *B. sauvagei*. In some areas these two species live sympatrically. In this species the males are very aggressive towards one another. They are, however, quite tolerant of *B. sauvagei* and *B. septuiclavis*. The males of *B. cyclura, B. crassicollis*, and *B. montana* will not tolerate one another. The incubation of the eggs and the rearing of the young do not present any problems.
Food: Waxmoth larvae, crickets, small locusts, moths, mealworms, banana, baby food on a banana base.

Bavayia sauvagei (Boulenger, 1833)

Distribution: New Caledonia.
Habitat: During the day beneath rocks or fallen timber in the rain forests. At night on low bushes.
Size: 110 mm.
Characteristics: The structure and patterning of this gecko are variable. The ground colour can vary from yellowish-brown to greyish-brown. Across the body there are large, light wave-like patches. These are partially edged in dark brown. In between there are irregular dark brown patches and stripes which extend over the entire body to the tip of the tail. The underside is unicoloured with light pigmentation at the edges. The males are easily recognised by their enlarged hemipenes pockets.

Bavayia sauvagei.

Vivarium: Type IV. The substrate must be kept moist. On this several
pieces of cork bark should be placed as hides. Thin branches and plants
will be used at night for climbing.

Husbandry and reproduction: A vivarium measuring $0.4 \times 0.3 \times 0.5$ m =
0.06 m^3 is adequate for a group of 12 animals. Hiding places should be
available on the ground. Several animals will often sleep together. A
limited number of pairs can be kept in a large vivarium, but if space is
limited the males can cause serious injuries to one another. Several
times each year the females lay two soft-shelled eggs which are buried.
After hatching the young measure 48–50 mm. The eggs should be
hatched in an incubator because the parents will readily eat the young.
Rearing the young presents no problems. They should be fed on fruit
flies, small waxmoth larvae, and banana. They must be given calcium
from hatching onwards. This will be willingly taken. These animals

Bavayia septuiclavis.

should be kept at temperatures of 25 °C during the day and 20 °C at night. In New Caledonia these geckoes are still active at a night temperature of 10 °C. A short reduction in the temperature is therefore not dangerous.

Food: Crickets, small locusts, waxmoth larvae, fruit flies, banana, and baby food on a banana base.

Similar species: *B. septuiclavis*. This species was only assigned to the genus *Bavayia* in 1989.

Diplodactylus (Gray, 1832)

This is a genus of geckoes which lives on the ground and amongst low bushes. There are 36 species, making this the largest group of Australian geckoes. They are small to medium-sized animals, the smallest of which is *D. elderi* at 45 mm, and the largest *D. ciliaris* with a head-rump length of 35 mm. Because of the large number of species, divergently coloured animals have evolved. For example, *D. taenicauda* is one of the most beautiful of the nocturnal geckoes. Some animals have even evolved special adaptations to their habitat. For instance, *D. elderi, D. mc. milliani* and *D. taeniatus* live amongst large clumps of grass. All species prefer dry to semi-dry desert areas.

The sexes are easily distinguished by the well-developed hemipenes pockets of the males. Some species have glands on the tail. These can emit an evil-smelling secretion. In the case of *Diplodactylus ciliaris* it is known that this secretion can be sprayed up to a distance of 50 cm.

Diplodactylus conspicillatus (Lucas & Frost, 1897)

Distribution: Australia.
Habitat: A terrestrial species which can be found in deserts as well as dry woodland and in stony areas.
Size: 80 mm.
Characteristics: These geckoes vary considerably in colour. The upper side of the body is mostly a reddish-brown with irregular darker spots. The underside is a whitish-pink without markings. The snout is very pointed with a very small mouth which is an indication of a specialist feeder. The tail is flat and at least as wide as the body. It is relatively short and ends in a small point.
Vivarium: Type I. The animals spend the day beneath rocks or in previously prepared hollows.
Husbandry and reproduction: The most difficult problem with these geckoes is to get them accustomed to different food. In the wild they probably eat termites, but in captivity they will only eat very small waxmoth larvae and fruit flies. However, amongst geckoes there are always individuals as far as food is concerned, and new sorts of food should always be offered, such as minute crickets and locusts from which the hind legs have been removed. Breeding has been achieved. The soft-shelled eggs were buried in a moist place in the vivarium and were hatched in an incubator. In this, the eggs were placed in moist vermiculite and kept at around 28 °C. The young hatched after 65 days and were around 25 mm long.
Food: Only the most minute insects, waxmoth larvae, wingless fruitfly, crickets, and springtails.

Diplodactylus conspicillatus.

Similar species: *Rhynchoedura ornata*. Both species live sympatrically and prefer the same food.

Diplodactylus steindachneri (Boulenger, 1885)

Distribution: Australia.
Habitat: A terrestrial animal which is often found on hard, stony ground. These geckoes live in the semi-arid deserts of Australia.
Size: 100 mm.
Characteristics: The dark brown to reddish-brown colour on the upper side of the body is interrupted by large beige-brown markings. Between these there are further spots and stripes. The underside is uniformly white and is sharply delineated laterally to the upper side of the body.
Vivarium: Type I. The substrate should be a loam/sand mixture and

Diplodactylus steindachneri.

should be quite compact. Because these geckoes do not burrow, all hollows will immediately be utilised as hiding places.

Husbandry and reproduction: These geckoes have only rarely been bred in captivity. To lay their soft-shelled eggs the females need a moist spot in the vivarium. A potted plant is readily accepted. The eggs should be transferred to an incubator. It has been found that after a few days the eggs should not be turned. If the position of the egg is altered the embryo dies. The young are always the same colour as the parents. The 60 mm young hatch after 60–75 days at a temperature of 28 °C and can be reared on small waxmoth larvae, newly hatched crickets, and wingless fruitfly. With good feeding the young can become sexually mature after 12–15 months. Males are easily recognised by their well-developed hemipenes pockets.

Food: Small crickets, small locusts, waxmoth larvae.

Similar species: *Diplodactylus byrnei, D. tessellatus, D. vittatus*.

Diplodactylus taenicauda.

Diplodactylus taenicauda (De Vis, 1886)

Distribution: Australia.
Habitat: These animals live on trees and bushes in the semi-arid bush-
land of eastern Australia. At night they are often found on the ground.
Size: 120 mm.
Characteristics: This gecko has a light beige ground colour with scattered irregular black spots. From the final vertebra there is a yellow or
red stripe running to the tip of the tail. The eyes are either red or green
according to the population from which the animal originates.
Vivarium: Type III. A well-compacted layer of sand/loam mixture
should be used as substrate. Some bushy plants and branches upon
which the geckoes may climb should also be placed in the vivarium.
Upright cork-bark tubes will be accepted as hiding places.
Husbandry and reproduction: See *Diplodactylus steindachneri*. Take
care when housing *Diplodactylus* species together. They are so closely

related that intergrades are easily produced. In this way, intergrades of
D. williamsi and *D. taenicauda* were produced in our vivaria.
Food: Small crickets, small locusts and waxmoths.
Similar species: *D. intermedius, D. strophurus, D. williamsi.*

Eurodactylodes (Wermuth, 1965)

The species *E. symmetricus* and *E. vieillardi* occur exclusively in New
Caledonia. In the wild they live amongst low bushes. When in danger
these species emit an evil-smelling secretion from the tail. It would
appear that there are glands between the segments of the tail, similar
to some *Diplodactylus* species. If slight pressure is exerted on the tail,
the secretion is sprayed for a distance of up to 30 cm. The two species
are differentiated by the length of the mouth opening. *E. symmetricus* opens its mouth up to the ear orifice. whilst in *E. vieillardi* it is
much shorter. In addition, *E. symmetricus* remains somewhat smaller
in size.

Eurodactylodes vieillardi (Bavay, 1869)

Distribution: New Caledonia.
Habitat: These geckoes live amongst low bushes in the rain forest.
Size: 130 mm.
Characteristics: With a total length of 130 mm, 65 mm is tail, which is
somewhat flattened on both the upper and underside. The entire tail
consists of segments around 1 mm wide. Between these and on the
sides of the tail it would appear that there are glands which emit an
evil-smelling secretion. For geckoes, these animals have a very unusual
scalation. The upper side of the body and head region are covered with
large, plate-like scales which do not touch one another and are separated by the skin between them. The almost white underside has normal scalation. According to their disposition and the background, the
animals can change from almost black to yellowish-grey. The mucous
membranes and tongue are bright yellow.
Vivarium: Type IV. In accordance with their natural habitat, several
branches and bushy plants should be placed in the vivarium. Suitable
plants are *Ficus benjamina* and *Euphorbia pulcherrima*. High atmospheric humidity is imperative.

Eurodactylodes symmetricus.

Husbandry and reproduction: Because this is not an aggressive species
it is possible to keep a large group together. However, the vivarium
should be well planted so that the animals are not always in sight of
one another. Their behaviour is very peaceful because they rely solely
on their camouflage. From September to November the females bury
their soft-shelled eggs in the moist substrate. When laid, the eggs measure 13 × 6 mm and grow to 17 × 11 mm shortly before hatching. The
50 mm young are not molested by the adults. With adequate feeding of
minute insects (Drosophila or waxmoth larvae) they can easily be
reared alongside the adults. The young are sexually mature after
around 18 months. The males may be recognised by the enlarged
hemipenes pockets.
Food: Crickets, small locusts, waxmoths, fruitfly, banana, baby food on
a banana base.

Hoplodactylus (Fitzinger, 1843)

The ten species of this genus have produced the largest gecko. *Hoplodactylus delcourti* was introduced to science by Bauer and Russel in
1986, in the form of a laboratory preparation from the Musée d'His-
toire Naturelle (Museum of Natural History) in Marseille. With a
head-rump length of 370 mm and a total length of over 600 mm the
size of this gecko is much greater than any other species. There does
however remain the question of whether geckoes of this species still
exist in the tropical forests of New Zealand. At the present time only
the species *H. duvaucelii* reaches a length of over 200 mm. The remainder are considerably smaller. Whilst the species *H. granulatus* and
H. maculatus have extended from the North to the South Island of
New Zealand, the species *H. pacificus* has not yet reached the South
Island. All other species only have a very small distribution range. One
of the most beautiful species lives only on the Stewart Islands to the
south of New Zealand. This is the very rare *Hoplodactylus rakiurae*. All
species are extremely delicate.

Hoplodactylus granulatus (Gray, 1895)

Distribution: New Zealand.
Habitat: These animals live on trees and shrubs in the forests.

Hoplodactylus granulatus.

Size: 190 mm.

Characteristics: Along the yellowish-grey to silver-grey back there are dark, wave-like transverse bands. The colours impinge on one another giving the impression that the animals are covered in lichens and mosses. They have orange-yellow mucous membranes and a yellow tongue. The toes have slightly developed clinging lamellae and at the end of each toe there is a strong claw. The tail can be used as an additional prehensile organ.

Vivarium: Type IV. For this species a densely planted vivarium is essential so that they can not see one another. In this way, large groups may be kept together. The height of the vivarium must be at least 60 cm, producing a space of 0.25 m^3 which is sufficient for four animals.

Husbandry and reproduction: It is only in a densely planted vivarium that several males may be kept together, otherwise these animals become very timid. Aggression is very rare. A 6–8 week rest period at temperatures of 10–15 °C stimulates mating. *H. granulatus* gives birth to live young. The young are born in May and measure around 60 mm. So that their progress may be regularly checked, the young should be reared singly.

Food: Field crickets, house crickets, waxmoths, waxmoth larvae, flies, banana, and banana-based baby food.

Similar species: *H. maculatus and H. pacificus.*

Naultinus (Gray, 1842)

This genus is represented on the North Island of New Zealand by two species. Whilst *N. grayi* is at home on the extreme north of the island, *N. elegans* can be found in the centre of the island. On the southeast of the island the subspecies *N. elegans punctatus* can be found. Each of the species is diurnal and is closely related to the likewise diurnal genus *Heteropholis* which occurs on the South Island of New Zealand. Like those they also give birth to live young.

Naultinus elegans (Gray, 1842)

Distribution: North Island of New Zealand.

Habitat: Low bushes in Manuka and Kanuka scrubland (similar to European cypress bushes).

Size: 150 mm.

Characteristics: Some animals are green without markings, whilst others have whitish-yellow spots and stripes on the upper side of the body. These are diurnal geckoes. They have a round eye with an oval pupil. The feet have only poorly developed clinging lamellae whilst the claws are very well developed. The tail which is circular in cross section can also be used as an additional prehensile organ. The mucous membranes are blue.

Vivarium: Type III. A densely planted vivarium is extremely important. Suitable plants are *Polyscias* and indoor cypresses. Several stout branches should be provided and the vivarium should be sprayed daily. No part of the vivarium however should be completely wet. A ventilator blowing occasionally into the vivarium provides the necessary fresh air.

Husbandry and reproduction: A group of *Naultinus elegans* can be kept

Naultinus elegans.

together in a densely planted vivarium. Even two males can be kept together but they must not be able to see one another constantly. It has been proved that by constant eye contact the dominant male can supress the others. Being kept in an outdoor vivarium during the summer months is beneficial. Temperatures below 10 °C have a positive effect on subsequent mating. The females are gravid for around 11 months. Because this species is ovo-viviparous the young are born live with a length of around 62 mm. In New Zealand the young are usually born in September or October, but in the vivarium this can vary considerably. From birth, the colouring of the young is identical to that of the parents.

Food: Field and house crickets (locusts are not normally eaten), waxmoths and their larvae, fruit flies, banana, and banana-based baby food.

Similar species: All species of this genus.

Nephrurus (Günther, 1876)

All seven species of this genus are at home on the Australian conti-
nent. Because the tail ends in a slight swelling this genus has been
given the common name "Button-Tailed Gecko." With the exception
of *N. asper* all other species live in dry, desert-like areas. *N. asper* also
lives in moist rain forest areas. They are exclusively terrestrial and usually spend most of the day in holes which they dig themselves. Temperature measurements taken at the habitat of *N. levis levis* gave
ground temperatures of 31 °C in the shade at 1:00 p.m. and 17 °C at
midnight. At a depth of 40 cm below ground the temperature was constant at 21 °C. At this depth the sand is always moist and the animals'
burrows usually end here. For species such as *N. laevissimus* or *N. stel-
latus* it is vital that their skin always comes into contact with a moist
substrate. All species usually remain below a length of 10 cm. The sexes
are easily distinguished by the well-developed hemipenes pockets of
the males. Because of the inaccessible terrain of some of the Australian desert regions it can safely be assumed that some species have still
not been discovered. Thus *N. deleani* was only described by Harvey in
1983. Some species have been bred through several generations in the
vivarium.

Nephrurus asper (Günther, 1876)

Distribution: Australia.
Habitat: A terrestrial species which occurs in desert regions as well as
deciduous forests. It is therefore important to know the origins of the
animals.
Size: 120 mm.
Characteristics: According to their biotope, the colouring of these animals can be very divergent. In the interior of Australia there are red
populations whilst normally the animals only vary from greyish-
brown to blackish-brown. Across the body there are narrow, wave-like,
beige-coloured transverse bands. The entire body is covered with spinous scales. The tail ends in a globule.
Vivarium: Type I or Type III. Because this species does not dig, the animals must be provided with hiding places in which they may stand upright.

Nephrurus asper.

Husbandry and reproduction: A ground area of 0.25 m² is adequate for a group of 12 animals. In the vivarium the animals mate several times in September and October and the eggs are laid in March or April of the following year. The females use their hind legs to roll the eggs in the sand until they are totally covered by substrate after which the 15 cm deep hole which has been excavated for oviposition is covered. The female seeks out a suitable laying site some days before the eggs are due and will inevitably choose a moist place in the vivarium. When laid the eggs measure 27 × 14 mm and grow to 30 × 16 mm during incubation. With the eggs laid in moist vermiculite and an incubation temperature of 28 °C the young hatch after 90–100 days. The newly hatched young measure around 50–55 mm and immediately after hatching have very imposing defensive behaviour. They raise the body, open the mouth wide, and hiss loudly at any adversary. Sometimes they will even spring towards their attacker. The adults can inflict an extremely painful bite.

Food: Locusts, crickets, grasshoppers, springtails, waxmoth larvae, cockroaches, pink mice.

Nephrurus levis (De Vis, 1886)

Distribution: Australia.

Habitat: These animals live in the desert regions in the interior of Australia. They spend the daytime in holes some 40 cm deep. These they dig themselves and at this depth the sand is constantly moist.

Size: 120 mm.

Characteristics: These geckoes have a large round head which is well set-off from the body. They are a pale pinkish-brown to dark lilac-brown. There are several grey to cream-coloured transverse bands across the front of the body. The first band is at the back of the head, the second on the neck and the third across the shoulders. There can be further bands across the body. The underside is uniformly white. At its root the tail can be quite wide and it ends in a nodule.

Vivarium: Type I. A deep layer of sand is essential and the lower reaches of this sand layer should be kept constantly moist. These geckoes dig their own burrows and for this reason it is important that the sand contains a certain degree of moisture.

Husbandry and reproduction: One male may be kept with several females. This depends largely upon the available ground area. For three animals this should not be less than 0.25 m². A gravid female becomes very restless shortly before the eggs are to be laid. At this time they are also often active during the day and frequently dig exploratory holes until they find a suitable place. The 27 × 15 mm eggs are then buried. The eggs continue to grow and shortly before hatching reach 30 × 20 mm. At around 28 °C the young hatch after 70–80 days measuring 50–60 mm. Immediately after being laid the eggs should be transferred to an incubator and placed in moist vermiculite for hatching. The young are difficult to rear. Here too it is important that part of the rearing container is kept moist. The young should be fed on small waxmoth larvae and hatchling crickets. All food should be liberally coated with calcium powder.

Nephrurus levis.

<u>Food:</u> Crickets, small locusts, grasshoppers, waxmoth larvae, spring-tails, mealworms, pink mice.

<u>Similar species:</u> *N. deleani, N. laevissimus, N. stellatus, N. vertebralis.*

Oedura (Gray, 1842)

The 13 species of this genus are all endemic to the Australian conti-nent. If they are fed too well, any food which is not immediately re-quired by the body can be stored in the fat tail, which gives rise to the very apt common name "Fat-Tailed Gecko". These geckoes are tree or rock-dwellers although some species, such as *Oedura castelnaui* and *Oedura coggeri*, can even be found in the rain forests. In comparison, the species *O. reticulata* and *O. marmorata* prefer arid regions. All ani-mals of this genus have well-developed clinging lamellae on the toes as well as retractile claws. They can negtiate perpendicular glass without problem. Because of their somewhat flattened body they are able to creep through gaps of less than 1 cm. Some species have only recently been introduced to science. For example *O. filicipoda, O. gracilis,* and *O. obscura* were only described as recently as 1984 by King, whilst King & Gow described *O. gemmata* in 1983. Care must be taken when keeping the various species together. In our experience the degree of

Oedura castelnaui.

relationship of one species to another can be determined by the degree of aggression between males. Males of *O. castelnaui* and *O. marmorata* will attack one another, as will males of *O. tryoni* and *O. monilis*. The latter two species will also interbreed. In comparison, the species *O. robusta* and *O. castelnaui* will live together quite peacefully. However, if possible, species of the same genus should not be kept together.

Oedura castelnaui (Thominot, 1889)

Distribution: Australia.
Habitat: This species leads an arboreal lifestyle, but some individuals have been found amongst rocks. They live in areas of high atmospheric humidity.
Size: 170 mm.
Characteristics: Characteristic of *O. castelnaui* are the sickle-shaped bands running transversely across the body. On the tail, which can be very flat, there are further bands. The colour spectrum ranges from dark grey to light yellow with a pinkish sheen. The underside is light beige.
Vivarium: Type III. The substrate should be loam to maintain high atmospheric humidity and several vertical branches should be installed. Cork-bark tubes or arches serve as hiding places.

Oedura leseurii.

Husbandry and reproduction: These geckoes are best kept in pairs or one male with two females. Males will fight amongst one another. The vivarium should be sprayed daily to guarantee adequate atmospheric humidity. The females bury their soft-shelled eggs in the moist earth beneath rocks or cork bark. After 65 to more than 80 days, the young hatch measuring around 60 mm. Rearing the young on small crickets and waxmoth larvae presents no problems and with good feeding the young can become sexually mature after only 1 year.
Food: Crickets, small locusts, waxmoth larvae, mealworms, springtails.
Similar species: *Oedura coggeri.*

Oedura leseurii (Dumeril & Bibron, 1836)

Distribution: Australia.
Habitat: Rocks overgrown with lichens. During the day beneath flat rocks or in rock crevices. They have the most southerly distribution

range of all *Oedura* species. Heavy rains and temperatures below 10 °C
are not uncommon.
Size: 100 mm.
Characteristics: These geckoes have brown and grey shades. Along the
back and down to the tip of the tail there is a grey, rhomboid-shaped
marking. Alongside this there are irregular spots.
Vivarium: Type V. Flat rocks should be stacked on one another and
some large angular rocks should also be placed in the vivarium. A ce-
mented rear wall has proved to be expedient. Loam is a suitable substrate.
Husbandry and reproduction: The temperature should not exceed
30 °C. A short period at a reduced temperature of below 10 °C stimulates mating. Regular spraying provides the necessary atmospheric humidity which is essential for these animals. The soft-shelled eggs are
buried in the moist substrate. Two days after hatching, the 5 cm long
young will eat small crickets and waxmoth larvae. It is imperative that
all food be liberally coated with calcium.
Food: Crickets, waxmoth larvae, small locusts, mealworms.

Oedura marmorata (Gray, 1842)

Distribution: Australia.
Habitat: These creatures prefer to live on dead trees, especially those
lying on the ground. Here they spend the day beneath loose bark. They
live in arid to semi-arid regions.
Size: 160 mm.
Characteristics: There are many different variations in the markings.
Some animals have light-beige to yellowish transverse bands on a dark
brown background. Between the bands there are irregular yellow
flecks. In some animals the transverse bands are absent, but the entire
body is marbled with yellow flecks. The intensity of the colouring varies even within one population.
Vivarium: Type III. The substrate can be sand. Several branches placed
at an angle and cork bark tubes will be immediately utilised by these
geckoes. Part of the vivarium should be kept permanently moist whilst
the remainder should be perfectly dry.
Husbandry and reproduction: In the wild these geckoes live in pairs on

Oedura marmorata.

one tree. Occasionally they will tolerate the presence of an individual juvenile animal. Two males will not tolerate one another. In the wild the females lay their soft-shelled eggs from the beginning of September until the end of November. These are buried in the moist earth. During the breeding season, two eggs will be laid every 4 weeks until 4–5 clutches have been produced. Once the females become accustomed to their vivarium, eggs will also be laid outside this period. The moist place in the vivarium will always be used for oviposition. For this, potted plants and bowls of moist loam may also be installed. The young hatch after 90–100 days at an incubation temperature of around 28 °C and measure some 7 cm. With good feeding they can reach sexual maturity within 1 year. The males may be recognised by their enlarged hemipenes pockets. Calcium is not eaten nor is fruit, and therefore all food should be liberally coated with calcium.

Food: Crickets, small locusts, waxmoths, waxmoth larvae, mealworms, springtails.

Similar species: *Oedura monolis, Oedura rhombifer.*

Phyllurus (Schinz, 1822)

All four species are endemic to Australia. They only occur in damp areas with frequent rainfall. Whilst the species *Phyllurus caudiannulatus* and *Phyllurus cornutus* live exclusively on trees, the species *Phyllurus platurus* and *Phyllurus salebrosus* can be found on cliffs. With a total length of 20 cm the latter is also the largest of all Australian geckoes. Because of their excellent camouflage it is very difficult to find these animals. They are very peaceful and rely totally on their camouflage. In the vivarium the temperature should not exceed 30 °C. All species are relatively flat with an even flatter tail. With the exception of *Phyllurus caudiannulatus*, the common name of "Leaf-Tailed Gecko" is very appropriate.

Phyllurus platurus (Shaw, 1970)

Distribution: Australia.
Habitat: These geckoes live amongst sandstone rocks in forest areas. They spend the daylight hours in rock crevices or beneath flat rocks. Day-long rainfall is not uncommon and the temperature sometimes drops to 0 °C.
Size: 160 mm.
Characteristics: A beige-brown colouring with dark brown pigmentation. The entire body in covered in spinous scales. The original tail is heart-shaped with a row of 2 mm spines along each side. A regenerated tail does not have these spines. The feet do not have clinging lamellae and end in well-developed claws.
Vivarium: Type V. Frequent spraying is essential and the temperature should never exceed 30 °C.
Husbandry and reproduction: These animals may be kept in groups. The males are not particularly aggressive towards one another and are easily distinguished by their well-developed hemipenes pockets. A cool period of 4–6 weeks at a temperature around 10 °C stimulates later mating activity. In the vivarium the eggs are laid from May to July. With an incubation temperature of 25 °C reduced to 20 °C at night the eggs hatch after 85–98 days. When the eggs are fertile a considerable increase in volume can be noticed during their development. Shortly

Phyllurus platurus.

before the eggs hatch they reach a size of 23 × 14 mm. The newly hatched young measure around 56 mm. The rearing container should contain stacked flat rocks.
Food: Waxmoth larvae, crickets, small locusts, mealworms, assorted beetles. All food should be liberally coated with calcium powder.
Similar species: *Phyllurus salebrosus*.

Pseudothecadactylus (Brongersma, 1934)

The two species of this genus are robust animals which grow to around 20 cm. Each species prefers a different habitat. *P. australis* is purely arboreal whilst *P. lindneri* can be found on cliffs. High atmospheric humidity is essential for both species. When well fed these animals lay in a layer of fat along both sides of the body. The males are easily recognised by the well-developed hemipenes pockets. Both species can inflict a very painful bite.

Pseudothecadactylus lindneri.

Pseudothecadactylus lindneri (Cogger, 1975)

Distribution: Northern Australia.

Habitat: These geckoes live on large sandstone cliffs. The daylight hours are spent in rock crevices or beneath loose flat rocks.

Size: 200 mm.

Characteristics: There are brown and yellow transverse bands over the whole of the upper body and down to the tip of the tail. The tail is relatively slender. Excess fat is stored in a wide fold on each side of the body. The underside is uniformly grey. The retractile claws are contained in a pocket on each toe.

Vivarium: Type V. For these animals high atmospheric humidity is absolutely essential.

Husbandry and reproduction: This species should be kept in pairs. Males will attack one another and can cause severe injuries. They may be kept with *Phyllurus platurus*. The soft-shelled eggs are buried in the moist substrate. To date however, no young have been hatched in captivity; several well-developed young died shortly before hatching, but the reason for this is not yet known. The husbandry of these animals presents no problems. One pair has been kept in captivity for 12 years. Food: crickets, small locusts, waxmoth larvae, moths in general, springtails.

Rhacodactylus (Fitzinger, 1843)

Apart from *Rhacodactylus auriculatus* which spends quite a considerable time on the ground, all other species are purely arboreal. In no other genus of gecko are there so many different ways of reproduction: *R. auriculatus*, *R. leachianus*, and *R. sarasinorum* lay soft-shelled eggs; *R. chahoua* lays eggs with such a thick layer of external calcium that they stick together and form double-eggs; whilst *R. trachyrhynchus* gives birth to live young. The method of reproduction of *R. ciliatus* is not yet known. All six species occur on New Caledonia and on the Loyalty Islands.

Rhacodactylus chahoua (Bavay, 1869)

Distribution: New Caledonia.
Habitat: These animals live on trees near streams and rivers, signifying that high atmospheric humidity is important.
Size: 250 mm.
Characteristics: The colouring consists of various brown and grey tones which run into one another. They frequently have a lichen-like pattern on the neck and tail. Tailless animals are not rare in the wild.
Vivarium: Type III. See *R. leachianus*.
Husbandry and reproduction: One male may be kept together with several females. Males, which can be recognised by their well-developed hemipenes pockets, will not tolerate one another. The females bury their eggs 5–10 cm deep in the moist substrate. Because of the thick external layer of calcium the eggs do not increase in size, but tend rather to split longitudinally. Beneath the calcium layer there is the elastic egg membrane. It is vital that the eggs do not dehydrate and for that reason it has proved to be expedient to place them in moist vermiculite for incubation at a temperature of 28 °C. The young hatch after 72–81 days and measure 90–110 mm. With good feeding the young can reach sexual maturity within 1 year.
Food: Field crickets, house crickets, small locusts, waxmoth larvae,

springtails, mealworms. Some specimens will also eat nestling mice. Bananas and banana-based baby food will be relished by all species.
Similar species: *Rhacodactylus sarasinorum, Rhacodactylus auriculatus.*

Rhacodactylus leachianus (Cuvier, 1829)

Distribution: New Caledonia.
Habitat: These animals live mainly in the crowns of dead trees. They lead a purely arboreal lifestyle.
Size: 360 mm.
Characteristics: The colouring consists of brown and green tones which run together to create a bark-like pattern. This species is distinguished by the short, set-off tail caused by a skin-fold on the body.
Vivarium: Type III. Because they live in the crowns of trees some 30 m high they are exposed to the heavy rainfall of these areas and because of the constant wind, the atmospheric humidity is always high. Frequent spraying is therefore vital and a ventilator should provide the necessary movement of air. The height of the vivarium should be at least 1 m and several thick branches should be provided. Large bird nesting boxes make suitable hiding places.
Husbandry and reproduction: These geckoes can only be kept singly or in pairs, and suitable pairs must first become accustomed to one another before breeding will take place. Great care must be taken when the animals are introduced. When a pair are established, the female lays eggs every 6–8 weeks during the period September–July. The eggs measure around 36×20 mm and are soft-shelled. They are buried 10 cm deep in the moist substrate. In the wild the eggs are laid in decaying branches and in rotting wood. In captivity, the eggs should be transferred to an incubator. At a temperature of 28 °C the 100 mm young hatch after 65–70 days. The young should be fed exclusively on waxmoth larvae. After 2 years the males can be recognised quite easily by their developing preanal pores.
Food: *Rhacodactylus leachianus* is very selective regarding food. In the early months the young feed only on waxmoth larvae. Later they will accept banana and banana-based baby food. After around 1 year mice and dog food will be taken. Take care when housing them with other lizards. Anything smaller than themselves will be immediately devoured.

Above: Rhacodactylus chahoua with a clutch of eggs.
Below: Two forms of Rhacodactylus leachianus.

SUBFAMILY GEKKONINAE (TRUE GECKOES)

Genera	Species	Distribution	Vivarium	Habitat
Afroedura	8	3c	II, III	B, D
Agamura	5	1a	II	D
Ailuronyx	2	7b, 7	III	B
Alsophylax	10	1, 3a	II, III	B, D
Ancylodactylus	1	3b	?	?
Aristelliger	4	4a, 4b	III	B
Asaccus	3	1a	II	D
Bogertia	1	4	?	?
Briba	1	4	?	?
Bunopus	4	1a	I	A
Calodactylodes	2	1b	III	A
Carinatogecko	2	1a		
Chondrodactylus	1	3c	I	A
Cnemaspis	21	1, 3	IV, V	B, D
Colopus	1	3c	II	A
Cosymbotus	2	1b, 1c	III	B
Crossobamon	1	1b	II	A
Cyrtodactylus	75	1, 6	II, III, IV	B, D
Dravidogecko	1	1b	?	?
Ebenavia	2	2, 7, 7a	IV	B
Garthia	2	4	?	?
Geckolepis	5	7	III	B
Geckonia	1	3a	I	A
Gehyra	30	1, 2, 9a	II, III	B, C
Gekko	21	1, 9a	III, IV	B, D
Gymnodactylus	2	4	III	B
Hemidactylus	71	worldwide	II, III	B, D
Hemiplyllodactylus	3	1, 9a	III	B
Heteronotia	2	2	I	A
Homonota	9	4, 4a, 4b	III	A
Homopholis	6	3, 7	III	B
Kaokogecko	1	3c	I	A
Lepidodactylus	22	1, 2, 8, 9, 9a	III	B
Luperosaurus	4	1c	?	?
Lygodactylus *	41	3, 7	III, IV, V	B, D
Millotisaurus	1	7	?	D

Genera	Species	Distribution	Vivarium	Habitat
Nactus	3	1, 2, 9, 9a	III	A
Narudasia	1	3c	II	A
Pachydactylus	34	3	II, III	A, D
Palmatogecko	1	3c	I	A
Paragehyra	1	7	?	?
Paroedura	8	7	II, III	A
Perochirus	3	1c, 9a	?	?
Phelsuma *	38	3b, 7–7c, 1c	III, IV	B
Pyhllodactylus	46	worldwide	I–V	A, B, C, D
Phyllopecus	1	4	?	?
Pristurus *	17	3a, 1a	II	A, B
Pseudogecko	1	1c	III	B
Ptenopus	3	3c	I	A
Ptychozoon	5	1c	III, IV	B
Pytodactylus	5	1a, 3a	II	D
Quedenfeldtia*	1	3a	II	D
Rhoptropella	1	3c	II	D
Rhoptropus *	7	3b, 3c	II	D
Saurodactylus	2	3a	I	A
Stenodactylus	12	1a, 3	I	A
Tarentola	14	3a, 4b, 6	II, III	B, D
Teratolepis	1	1a	I	A
Teratoscincus	4	1	I	A
Thecadactylus	1	4, 4a, 4b	III	B
Trachydactylus	1	3a	?	?
Tropiocolotes	9	1a, 3a	II	A
Uroplatus	8	7	IV	B
Wallsaurus	1	1c	?	?

* Denotes diurnal species

The subfamily Gekkoninae is distinguished by the fact that all animals of this genus lay hard-shelled eggs. Within this subfamily parthenogenic species have also developed.

The eggs are very resistant to external influences. They may be laid individually or adhering together as a double clutch. Mass laying sites are not uncommon. This subfamily contains the greatest number of species and has the largest distribution range. They occur in both the old and new worlds. Some genera have developed into diurnal species. In the table these are marked with an asterisk *.

Ailuronyx (Fitzinger, 1843)

The common name "Bronze Gecko" does not take into account the considerable variability of these animals. The basic tone of the colouring is however a yellowish-brown to bronze, but many specimens have white spots and stripes. To date the two species *A. seychellensis* and *A. trachygaster* have been scientifically described.

It has been discovered that two further forms exist (Henkel & Zobel, 1987). These two forms live sympatrically on the Seychelles Island of Praslin. It has also been proven that striped specimens of some forms can occur. *A. trachygaster* has not been rediscovered to date. This species, which supposedly comes from Madagascar, was described by Duméril in 1851.

Ailuronyx seychellensis (Duméril & Bibron, 1836)

Distribution: Seychelles.
Habitat: These animals live mainly on palm trees but are becoming followers of civilisation and are colonising the houses of the Seychelles Islanders.
Size: To date three different body sizes are known. The largest animals (250 mm) and the smallest (150 mm) live together on the island of Praslin. The medium-sized animal at 200 mm is known from the island of Mahé.
Characteristics: The animals are yellowish-brown to bronze in colour. Some animals have dorso-lateral stripes which can be black and white, as well as black and white spots. Characteristic of all species is the extreme delicacy of the skin. With only very slight pressure large areas of skin can be dislodged.
Vivarium: Type III. These animals make no great demands regarding their environment, but the conditions under which they are kept should not be too dry.
Husbandry and reproduction: It is best to keep these animals in pairs and even then some injuries caused by fighting can occur. The males may be recognised by their well-developed preanal pores. Pieces of

bamboo the thickness of a human arm and open at one end have proved most suitable for oviposition. The females affix their eggs to a solid surface and there are usually two eggs which are pressed against the solid surface until they harden. At a temperature of 28 °C the young hatch after around 90 days.

Food: Field crickets, house crickets, waxmoths and their larvae, spring-tails, mealworms, banana, and banana-based baby food.

Aristelliger (Cope, 1862)

The distribution range of this genus is limited to the Caribbean region. These geckoes live mainly on stout trees. They have a loud call which can be heard over a vast distance. It sounds like the cracking of nuts. The call is most frequently heard when the geckoes are being aggressive towards one another.

Aristelliger praesignis (Hallowell, 1857)

Distribution: Jamaica and the Cayman Islands.
Habitat: A completely arboreal species.
Size: 250 mm.
Characteristics: The ground colour is a dirty-grey to beige and the entire upper half of the body is covered with dark brown spots and stripes. Along the flanks there are irregular reddish-brown flecks. From the neck to the tip of the tail there are large light-beige to yellow shiny flecks. The clinging lamellae on the feet are well-developed, as are the prominent claws on each toe. Because of their poorly developed hemipenes pockets, the males are difficult to distinguish.
Vivarium: Type III. The vivarium should be sprayed at 2-day intervals.
Husbandry and reproduction: These animals are extremely aggressive towards one another, and even the females will attack, causing severe injuries to one another. For this reason only a single pair can be kept in each vivarium, and even then, sufficient hiding places must be provided. In captivity the females lay their eggs on the ground beneath bark or loam. The eggs should be hatched in an incubator because the adults will eat the young without hesitation.
Food: Field crickets, house crickets, waxmoth larvae, springtails, grasshoppers.

Above: The various patterns of Ailuronyx seychellensis.
Below: Aristelliger praesignis.

Chondrodactylus angulifer.

Chondrodactylus (Peters, 1870)

Chondrodactylus angulifer (Peters, 1870)

Distribution: South Africa.
Habitat: Arid to semi-arid desert regions.
Size: 180 mm.
Characteristics: A very compact terrestrial gecko, the ground colour of which can be reddish-brown to yellowish brown. Along the back there are wave-shaped dark-brown transverse bands. This pattern is especially pronounced in the young. The males are easily recognised by the well-developed hemipenes pockets and up to six white spots on each side of the spine.
Vivarium: Type I.
Husbandry and reproduction: A group of one male and up to four females may be kept in a vivarium with a ground area of 0.5 m². The females often spend the daylight hours together in one hiding place. Stacked flat rocks or cork tunnels make suitable hiding places. In captivity the females lay their eggs mainly during the months of January

to March. The eggs are laid beneath a pile of sand. These are very thin-shelled eggs which should be very carefully removed and transferred to an incubator. The eggs measure between 19 × 13 mm–22 × 17 mm. At a temperature of 28 °C and a relative atmospheric humidity of 75% the eggs hatch after 60–80 days producing young measuring 62–68 mm. The eggs should be placed on sand for incubation. The warning behaviour, which is very pronounced in the young, can be regarded as a sort of mimicry of scorpions. The tail is arched forward in the same way as a scorpion arches the sting, after which the gecko will often spring at its opponent. This tactic usually suffices as a shock and the gecko then retreats. Adults of this species can inflict an extremely painful bite.

Food: Field crickets, house crickets, small locusts, springtails, waxmoth larvae. Larger animals will also take pink mice.

Similar species: *C. a. namibensis*.

Cyrtodactylus (Gray, 1827)

This genus has produced more species than any other. Although there are a large number of species they have not yet reached the New World. Even in Australia, the species *C. louisiadensis* is only found in the extreme north. Although the Asiatic species live in moist biotopes, those from Asia Minor live in dry areas. More and more scientists tend to split the genus *Cyrtodactylus* into different genera. Thus a geographic separation into Palaeartic and Oriental species would appear to be sensible.

Cyrtodactylus caspius (Eichwald, 1831)

Distribution: Southern Russia, Iran, Afghanistan.

Habitat: Usually amongst rocks and in some places on house walls. Hibernation from October to March. Night temperatures below 10 °C are not uncommon.

Size: 160 mm.

Characteristics: The ground colour is light grey to grey-brown. Across the body and down to the tip of the tail there are several interrupted dark brown transverse bands. The toes end in a claw and have no clinging lamellae.

Vivarium: Type II. Plants are not neccessary and although these geckoes should be kept dry, light spraying each morning is advisable. During the day the temperature may safely reach 30 °C.
Husbandry and reproduction: Keeping one male with several females will present no problems. The males may be recognised by their preanal and femoral pores, which in comparison with those of the females are somewhat swollen and are brown in colour. A hibernation period of 4–6 weeks at a temperature of 10 °C is essential. After this these geckoes will normally mate immediately. Two hard-shelled eggs of 8 × 13 mm are laid and, after an incubation period of 55–70 days at 28 °C, the young hatch measuring some 50 mm. The colouring of the young is identical to that of the parents and rearing them presents no problems.
Food: Field crickets, house crickets, small locusts, waxmoths and their larvae, mealworms, flies, and other small insects.
Similar species: *C. fedtschenkoi, C. kotschyi.*

Cyrtodactylus peguensis (Boulenger, 1893)

Distribution: S. E. Burma, southern Thailand, northern Malaysia.
Habitat: Tropical rain forest. During the day the animals hide beneath leaf mould and dead trees.
Size: 150 mm.
Characteristics: According to their origins these animals are somewhat divergent in colour; the typical spotted pattern is not always present. The ground colour is always a yellowish-brown to chocolate-brown which is interspaced with wide yellow lines. The original tail is coloured totally differently; it is dark brown with notched beige rings.
Vivarium: Type IV. High atmospheric humidity is vital therefore the substrate should consist of a material which will retain moisture. A loam/sand mixture or potting compost are both suitable. Several hiding places should be provided. These geckoes are also great climbers.
Husbandry and reproduction: These geckoes do not need particularly high temperatures and will die above 30 °C. A temperature range between 20 and 26 °C appears to be ideal. One male and several females may be kept together without any problems. Hard-shelled eggs are laid throughout the year with the exception of occasional rest periods. The

Cyrtodactulus peguensis.

Cyrtodactylus pulchellus.

eggs measure 9 × 11 mm and great care should be taken when removing them because the shell is extremely thin. At a temperature of 28 °C the 55–60 mm young hatch after 70–80 days. High atmospheric humidity is essential for the development of the eggs. Males may be easily recognised by their enlarged hemipenes pockets. Sexual maturity may be reached in 1 year.

Food: Field crickets, house crickets, small locusts, mealworms, waxmoth larvae.

Cyrtodactylus pulchellus (Gray, 1928)

Distribution: N. E. India, Burma, Thailand, Malaysia.
Habitat: The rain forests of the Central Highlands above 1300 m. They are predominantly tree-dwellers but can also be found amongst rocks and on houses.
Size: 260 mm.

Characteristics: The ground colour goes from yellowish-brown to dark violet. From the back of the head and along the back there are wide transverse bands enclosed by white to yellowish lines composed of spots. The tail is dark brown with beige to white rings.
Vivarium: Type IV. Several thick branches should be installed and a high atmospheric humidity is very important. Temperature not above 30 °C (see *C. peguensis*).
Husbandry and reproduction: The incubation period of the eggs of this species is 140–209 days at 20–28 °C (Marronde, 1990), much longer than most other geckoes. The males may be easily recognised by their well-developed hemipenes pockets.
Food: Field crickets, house crickets, small locusts, beetles, waxmoths and their larvae.
Similar species: *C. marmoratus.*

Ebenavia (Boettger, 1878)

Only one species of this genus is known to date. It occurs only on Madagascar and the Comoros Islands.

Ebenavia inunguis (Boettger, 1878)

Habitat: The habitat of these creatures covers the most divergent forms of vegetation, from rain forest to dry forest and even on the savannahs. During the day they can be found beneath loose bark, especially in places warmed by the sun. They can also be found on cliffs and in rock crevices.
Size: 80 mm.
Characteristics: This is a small slender species, the head of which runs to a pointed snout. The scales are small and fine, and along each side of the tail there is a row of pointed scales. These geckoes vary greatly in colour. The ground colour can go from olive-green through beige to brown, but the animals always have a dark stripe. The patterning on the tail can also vary considerably. There are forms which have an orange-coloured side stripe.
Vivarium: Type IV. A suitable substrate is a mixture of sand and peat or potting compost. As hiding places, several pieces of bark should be

Ebenavia inunguis.

provided, affixed to the rear and side walls of the vivarium. Several climbing branches and some bushy plants complete the furnishings.

Husbandry and reproduction: These geckoes are extremely tolerant and peaceful and may therefore be kept in small groups. They are active at twilight and scurry around the vivarium in the search for food. Around 5 weeks after mating the females lay a single, hard-shelled egg which is hidden beneath leaf mould or moss. During the breeding season, from April to September, the females usually lay 4 eggs. These should be incubated at 25 °C and require around 65 days to hatch. Rearing the young presents no problems and they can reach sexual maturity in 1 year.

Food: Springtails, fruit flies, small crickets, and small waxmoth larvae.

Geckolepis (Grandidier, 1967)

Typical of this genus is the roof-tile-like scalation. When handled large sections of skin can be dislodged (see section on "Skin and Scalation"). Apart from *G. maculata*, which occurs on Grande Comore, all other species are found on Madagascar and the neighbouring islands. As a means of distinguishing the various species, Angel (1942) cites the different scalations of the lower jaw.

Geckolepis typica (Grandidier, 1867)

Distribution: Madagascar, Sainte Marie Island, and Ile aux Prunes.
Habitat: On trees and very frequently on the walls of the islanders' homes.
Size: 160 mm.
Characteristics: These animals have brown to bronze-coloured scales. Several scattered dark brown to black and sometimes even red scales give the animals a speckled appearance.
Vivarium: Type III. Upright pieces of cork bark provide the neccessary hiding places.
Husbandry and reproduction: The males can be recognised by their prominent hemipenes pockets, and one may be kept with several females. However, several hiding places must be provided because females will also occasionally fight amongst themselves. The two 14 × 12 mm eggs will be affixed to the rear of the cork bark. At a temperature of 25–30 °C the 45 mm young take around 40 days to hatch. Rearing the young presents no problems.
Food: Medium-sized crickets, small locusts, waxmoth larvae, banana, and banana-based baby food.
Similar species: *G. maculata*.

Geckonia (Mocquard, 1895)

Geckonia chazaliae (Mocquard, 1895)

Distribution: Northwest Africa.
Habitat: These animals only occur along the coast. Here they live amongst the vegetation on the sand dunes. They can also be found in rocky desert regions. During the day they can often be found beneath

Geckolepis maculata.

rocks and camel dung. The moisture found here, as well as the coastal
mists, are essential for the well-being of this genus.
Size: 95 mm.
Characteristics: The large head is well set-off from the body. At the
back of the head these animals have a slight swelling covered by thorn-
like scales. These give it its common name of "Helmeted Gecko". The
tail is short and thin. The colour is light grey to reddish-brown. A broken white line runs along the back to the tail joint. Dark brown spots
are irregularly scattered over the entire upper side of the body. The underside is uniformly white.
Vivarium: Type I. Part of the vivarium should be kept constantly moist,
and hiding places should be provided in both the dry and moist parts.
A localised temperature of 30 °C in the dry area is also equally impor-

Geckonia chazaliae.

tant. This can be achieved by placing a heating cable beneath the vivarium. Spraying the vivarium early in the morning will also contrib-
ute to the well-being of the animals.

Husbandry and reproduction: Several pairs may only be kept in a large
vivarium with a minimum floor area of 0.5 m². It is however advisable
to keep only one male with several females. During mating the males
regularly attack the females and hold them in position by a bite to the
neck. The 13 × 10 mm hard-shelled eggs are buried in the substrate. On
hatching the young measure around 40 mm but it is not advisable to
rear them alongside the adults. Although the young will not be attacked, they will find it difficult to compete for food. It is much better
to rear the young in individual small vivaria so that their progress may
be regularly checked. Even when several juveniles are reared together,
the older animals will oppress the younger ones. If fed well the young

can reach sexual maturity in 9–12 months. The males may be easily distinguished by their well-developed hemipenes pockets. Because of their excellent camouflage, these geckoes do not make any attempt to escape from a potential enemy. They usually remain motionless and press themselves against the substrate. A short winter rest period of 4 weeks at a temperature of 10 °C has a stimulating effect on subsequent mating.

Food: This species particularly enjoys woodlice. Other suitable foods are crickets, small locusts, mealworms, springtails, and waxmoth larvae.

Gehyra (Gray, 1834)

Several species of this genus are cosmopolitan. *G. multilata*, together with several *Hemidactylus* species, have colonised a worldwide distribution range. Because of their excellent adaptability they are found in many ports around the world. The hard-shelled eggs are very resistant to external influences. The colouring of these geckoes does not attract any attention. Most species are beige-grey to flesh-coloured and have a length of around 100–150 mm. Nevertheless there are species such as *G. oceanica* and *G. vorax* which can reach lengths in excess of 200 mm.

Gehyra dubia (MacLeay, 1877)

Distribution: Eastern Australia.
Habitat: Can be found on trees, as well as on rocks, in both moist and dry areas. Variable.
Size: 110 mm.
Characteristics: The ground colour is beige-grey. Dark brown to almost black spots and stripes are present over the entire body.
Vivarium: Type III. If the origin of the animals is not known it is best to keep them under somewhat dry conditions.
Husbandry and reproduction: During the day these animals hide beneath loose bark or below rocks. Males will fight amongst themselves. They may be recognised by their well-developed hemipenes pockets. In a large vivarium with many hiding places it is possible to keep several pairs together. The two 11 × 10 mm hard-shelled eggs are laid beneath rocks or bark. Moist warm places are preferred. Although some

Gehyra dubia.

parent geckoes will not attack their young, these will however be eaten by other adults. It is therefore advisable to rear the young separately. On hatching the young measure around 50 mm, and for the first weeks they should be fed on fruitflies, micro-crickets, and the smallest waxmoth larvae. The young of this species grow very quickly.

Food: Waxmoth larvae, crickets, small locusts, moths. Some species will also lick banana.

Similar species: Because the entire genus is so adaptable, most species may be kept under the same conditions.

Gekko (Laurenti, 1768)

The distribution of this species stretches from southeast Asia through Korea and Japan down to the Indo-Australian Archipelago. However, no species has yet reached Australia. In many areas these geckoes have adapted to the various environmental conditions and live as followers of civilisation in housing areas. They are mainly large species which can exceed a total length of 200 mm. With their strong jaws and very sharp teeth they can inflict an extremely painful bite. The large, undivided clinging lamellae give them an extremely firm grip.

Gekko gecko (Linnaeus, 1758)

Distribution: From N. E. India to the Indo-Australian Archipelago.
Habitat: In tropical rain forests, on cliffs and trees, and in increasing numbers amongst human habitation.
Size: 350 mm.
Characteristics: Numerous brownish-red to bright red spots and flecks on a grey background.
Vivarium: Type IV. Because of the size of these animals, the height of the vivarium should not be less than 1 m and the width not less than 0.8 m. Stout branches and cork bark tubes should be stood upright in the vivarium. Daily spraying is advisable.
Husbandry and reproduction: One male, which can easily be recognised by its angular row of preanal pores, may be kept with several females. For sexual attraction the males have a call which can be heard over a wide area; the call is a loud "to-kay" and is repeated several times. The female affixes the 18 × 20 mm eggs to a solid foundation where they are guarded by the parents. At a temperature of 25–30 °C incubation takes from 100–200 days. At lower temperatures incubation can take more than 200 days. The young hatch measuring around 100 mm. When disturbed the young will immediately seek protection from their parents. The adults actually protect their young. Juveniles which have been removed from the vivarium for a while (around one week) and which are then reintroduced will promptly be eaten. When sufficient insects are available for them the young may be reared with the adults.
Food: Springtails, mealworms, cockroaches, crickets, grasshoppers, pink mice, locusts.

Gekko monarchus (Dumérril & Bibron, 1836)

Distribution: Southern Thailand, Malaysia, Phillipines, Indo-Australian Archipelago.
Habitat: A tree-dwelling species which is also frequently found on houses.
Size: 200 mm.
Characteristics: Along the spine there are pairs of dark brown to black spots on a brown background.

Gekko monarchus.

Vivarium: Type IV. Furnished as for *Gekko gecko*.
Husbandry and reproduction: Both sexes have an angular row of pre-
anal pores, but those of the males are more prominent. Two eggs are
affixed to a solid foundation. The 80 mm young hatch after 100 days.
The young must be separated from the parents or they will be eaten.
Food: See *Gekko gecko*.

Gekko vittatus (Houttuyn, 1782)

Distribution: Indo-Australian Archipelago from Java to Oceania.
Habitat: A tree-dwelling species which on some islands can also be
found in houses.
Size: 250 mm.

Gekko vittatus.

Characteristics: The ground colour is a yellowish-brown to dark brown. A white stripe runs from behind the eyes and over the ear orifice to the neck. There both stripes meet and run as a central line to the start of the tail. The tail has several white rings. These are very slender animals.

Vivarium: Type III. The height of the vivarium should not be less than 60 cm. Stout branches and robust plants complete the furnishings. An atmospheric humidity of 75% should be maintained.

Husbandry and reproduction: These animals may be kept in groups of one male and up to three females provided the vivarium is large enough. The females are not aggressive towards one another. This species also affixes its eggs, usually two, to a smooth surface, often choosing the glass at the front of the vivarium. The eggs may be incubated

in the vivarium and the young will not be in any danger from the adults. At a temperature of 23–28 °C the young hatch after 70–80 days. It is better to rear the young separately so that their progress may be regularly checked. These geckoes do not pose any problems.
Food: See *Gekko gecko.*

Hemidactylus (Oken, 1817)

Some of the approximately 65 species of the genus *Hemidactylus* (Half-Fingered Geckoes) are now distributed almost worldwide and can be found in the most divergent vegetation zones. These species are distinguished by their extreme adaptability, a reason why many of them have become followers of civilisation.

Hemidactylus frenatus (Duméril & Bibron, 1836)

Distribution: Originally Asia, nowadays cosmopolitan.
Habitat: Because of their adaptability very divergent. Some examples: beneath tree bark, in wall cavities, in houses and other buildings. In addition this species also occurs in the most divergent vegetation zones, such as rain forests, savannahs, and deserts.
Size: 140 mm.
Characteristics: The shape of the body is fairly uniform and the head is only slightly set-off from the body. The scalation too is quite uniform. The ground colour ranges from a matte grey or light brown through beige to a greenish irridescence. Most animals have some lighter flecks and wave-like stripes.
Vivarium: Type III. The substrate should be a shallow layer of sand. The rear and side walls should be covered with small rocks or cork bark. Several stout branches and a bushy plant complete the furnishings.
Husbandry and reproduction: *H. frenatus* is a very intolerant species and is best kept as individual pairs. In the wild the males at least have a strictly delineated territory which they defend vigourously. When housed with other species care should be taken that the other animals are not smaller. After a short courtship, during which the male repeatedly touches the female with his snout, mating takes place. Around 3–4 weeks later the female lays two hard-shelled eggs. These are partially

Hemidactylus frenatus.

fixed to a solid surface. At a temperature of 28 °C the 46–60 mm young hatch after 55–62 days. The young should be reared individually and separated from the adults. The young reach sexual maturity after 1 year. Under the same conditions in the vivarium, these geckoes will breed throughout the year.

Food: Field crickets, house crickets, small locusts, waxmoths and their larvae, springtails, and spiders.

Similar species: *H. brooki* from West Africa.

Hemidactylus mabouia (Moreau & Jonnés, 1818)

Distribution: Originally Africa, today worldwide.

Habitat: This species lives on cliffs, buildings, and trees.

Size: 180 mm.

Characteristics: The upper side is grey to grey-brown, sometimes also with a tinge of green. Along the back there is a pattern of dark flecks and transverse bands which often are not very noticeable.

Vivarium: Type III. This species makes no great demands regarding the vivarium. Suitable furnishings are a potted plant, several stout branches and some rocks or cork bark as hiding places.

Husbandry and reproduction: *H. mabouia* is also a very unsociable species which is best kept in pairs with other animals of a similar size. After mating the female lays two hard-shelled eggs inside a tree hollow or simply beneath loose bark. In the wild places can also be found where masses of eggs have been laid, which proves that although they defend a territory, they live in fairly dense populations. Incubation takes around 60 days at 26–30 °C. The young reach sexual maturity after 1 year and will then breed throughout the year.

Food: Field crickets, house crickets, small beetles, springtails, and spiders.

Similar species: *H. flaviviridis*.

Hemidactylus turcicus (Linnaeus, 1758)

Distribution: Originally in the Mediterranean area, in north Africa and southwest Asia. It has also been introduced into North and Central America.

Habitat: Frequently found on the walls of buildings and cliff faces, but rarely on trees.

Size: Up to 120 mm. European animals however only reach around 80 mm.

Characteristics: These animals are covered in small scales which are irregularly interrupted by tubercular scales. The ground colour is a grey, beige, or brown tone with irregular dark flecks. In addition there are several more-or-less predominant transverse bands along the back and tail.

Vivarium: Type II. A suitable substrate is a layer of sand 2 cm deep. The furnishings should consist of a potted plant as well as several flat, stacked rocks and upright rocks lying against the side and rear walls of the vivarium.

Husbandry and reproduction: *H. turcicus* too is a very unsociable species. Even when pairs are kept, aggression and fights may be expected.

The main criterion for breeding this species successfully is a pronounced variation of the temperature during the year. If possible the vivarium should be simply placed in a cool cellar for two months at a temperature of 15–18 °C and then reinstalled in the reptile room. After only a few days the territorial calls of the male will be heard late in the evening. Mating takes place after a further 4 weeks. From then onwards the female will lay 2–3 clutches every 4 weeks. The eggs are laid beneath rocks or are simply buried in the sand. At 25–28 °C incubation takes 50–55 days. The young are very small, only around 30 mm long and will immediately show their aggressive nature. They must be reared individually and separately from their parents. They reach sexual maturity after 2 years. During incubation it is essential that the eggs do not become wet.

Food: Field crickets, house crickets, waxmoths and their larvae, spiders, springtails, and other small insects.

Homopholis (Blaesodactylus) (Boulenger, 1895)

This genus was revised in 1980 by Böhme and Meier. With the description of a new species the three Madagascan species previously known as *Blaesodactylus* were reassigned to the genus *Homopholis* which had previously been known only from Africa. However, as a nomenclature, the name *Blaesodactylus* shall remain to indicate a subgenus within the genus. A total of six species have been described. The species *H. fasciata, H. mulleri,* and *H. wahlbergii* live in Africa whilst *H. antongilensis, H. boivini*, and *H. sakalava* can be found in Madagascar. Similar animals to *H. antongilensis* have been found in the northwest of Madagascar, however the difference in size is considerable. The unsociability of these animals is the same as for all other species. Even the females will inflict serious injuries on one another. It is known that the Madagascan species bury their eggs.

Homopholis antongilensis (Böhme & Meier, 1980)

Distribution: Eastern Madagascar.
Habitat: A tree-dwelling species from the eastern rain forests of Madagascar.
Size: 200 mm.

Characteristics: On a greyish-brown background there are wave-like transverse bands running to the tip of the tail. A broken white line runs along the spine interrupting the transverse bands. The entire body is covered with granular scales.
Vivarium: Type I. In accordance with the arboreal lifestyle of these geckoes, the vivarium should contain several stout branches. Frequent spraying is neccessary to maintain an atmospheric humidity above 75%.
Husbandry and reproduction: Only one pair may be kept in each vivarium because even the females will inflict serious injuries on one another. Whilst mating the females may also suffer injuries in the neck region because the males are particularly brutal towards the females. For oviposition the females use their hind legs to dig a hole in the ground. To do this they cling onto a tree trunk with their forelegs and use their hind legs as a sort of excavator. The 50 mm young hatch in the vivarium. They should be reared separately however, because they will be attacked by the parents.
Food: Beetles, field crickets, house crickets, small locusts, waxmoths and their larvae, moths, banana, and banana-based baby food.

Homopholis boivini (Duméril, 1856)

Distribution: Northern Madagascar.
Habitat: This species is found on trees, cliffs, and the walls of buildings. They live predominantly in the dry forest areas in the north of Madagascar.
Size: 300 mm.
Characteristics: These geckoes are a beige to grey colour without any prominent patterning. The entire upper side of the body is covered in small tubercular scales. The underside is white with small brown flecks. The amber-coloured eyes are surrounded by yellow circles.
Vivarium: Type II. To cater for the arboreal lifestyle of this species the vivarium should contain several stout branches. It is also important to provide a deep layer of sand in which the eggs will be laid. It is imperative that these geckoes be kept under dry conditions.
Husbandry and reproduction: This species appears to be the most un-

Homopholis antongilensis.

sociable of all, and will readily inflict severe injuries, therefore adequate hiding places should be provided. A pair which will tolerate one another should never be separated. This species buries its eggs in the same way as *H. antongilensis*. Rearing the young presents no problems. Care must be taken when attempting to remove the eggs from the vivarium. The young may be kept with the parents.
Food: Beetles, field crickets, house crickets, small locusts, grasshoppers, and other insects. Some individuals will also eat nestling mice.
Similar species: *Homopholis sakalava* may be kept under the same conditions.

Lepidodactylus (Fitzinger, 1843)

Apart from *Lepidodactylus lugubris* all other species are endemic to Asia and the Indo-Pacific region. They are mainly small geckoes measuring around 100 mm. As followers of civilisation they are frequently found on the walls of houses and other buildings.

Lepidodactylus lugubris (Duméril & Bibron, 1836)

Distribution: Over the whole of Asia, on the Indo-Australian Archipelago, in Oceania, New Zealand, Central America, South America.
Habitat: This species can be found from the coast into the deepest rain forest. They are predominantly tree-dwellers. As followers of civilisation they can also be found amongst human habitations.
Size: 90 mm.
Characteristics: The ground colour is a yellowish-brown. Along the spine and down to the tail there are pairs of dark brown to black spots. These can sometimes touch one another. The tail is somewhat flattened and has teeth-like scales along the sides.
Vivarium: Type II. Several branches and cork tubes are the only furnishings required. The vivarium should be sprayed every 2 days.
Husbandry and reproduction: The most interesting thing about this species is the method of reproduction. The animals are parthenogenic. The females lay 1 or 2 eggs every 2–4 weeks and these will usually be affixed to the front glass panel. According to the ambient temperature, the 35–37 mm young hatch after 60–100 days. Because these will once

Lepidodactylus lugubris.

again be all females, they can, provided they have been well fed, be expected to breed after 6–8 months. The reproductive capability of these
animals is enormous. Varied food which is regularly sprinkled with
calcium is extremely important. With sufficient hiding places and an
adequate supply of food, the young may be safely left with the adults.
This is an ideal species for the beginner.

Food: Waxmoth larvae, fruit flies, minute crickets and other small insects, sweet fruit, honey, and fruit-based baby food.

Lygodactylus (Gray, 1864)

This is a genus of diurnal geckoes whose members rarely exceed a
length of 100 mm. Their range of distribution is in tropical Africa and
nearby islands as well as Madagascar. Of over 40 species, the colouring

of the majority is fairly dull and consists of grey, brown, and beige patterns. A small number of species, for example *L. fischeri*, are green. Others are so well adapted to their habitat that they are extremely difficult to find, as is the case with *Lygodactylus spinulifer*, which only occurs in the rain forests of Madagascar. However, such extreme habitats as the Ankaratra Mountains of Madagascar, with an altitude of over 2000 m, are inhabited by the species *Lygodactylus arnoulti* together with the lesser known genus *Millotisaurus*. Here the animals hide in rock crevices and beneath loose rocks. When keeping *Lygodactylus* it is essential that the origin of the animal is known since the well-being of many species depends upon them being kept under conditions similar to those prevalent in their natural habitat.

Lygodactylus picturatus (Peters, 1896)

Distribution: East Africa; from Ethiopia to Mozambique, the Mafia Islands and Zanzibar, westwards towards Zaire.
Habitat: A purely arboreal species which lives at a height of 2–3 m above ground. These animals live in dry areas with afternoon temperatures above 40 °C in the shade. This is therefore obviously a gecko which needs a great deal of sunshine.
Size: 85 mm.
Characteristics: This species exhibits very pronounced sexual dimorphism. Whilst the females are mainly brown with some lighter flecks, the males have a bright yellow head and shoulder area with dark spots and stripes. The body legs and tail are a blueish-grey. The black throat is much more visible than the orange underside. The round pupils indicate that this is a diurnal species.
Vivarium: Type III. A dry vivarium without any rocks. Because these animals like to climb, several smooth, stout branches should be installed. These must always stand upright since the animals are accustomed to running around on tree trunks. A spotlight will provide a localised temperature increase to 35 °C. There should also be cooler places. The vivarium should be not less than 40 cm high, and taller than it is wide.
Husbandry and reproduction: These geckoes should be kept in pairs.

Lygodactylus picturatus.

The courtship behaviour of the males is identical to the warning displays performed before other males. The bright colours of the head,
throat, and shoulders, as well as the flattening of the body and sideways
movements are all part of both displays. It is the reaction of the other
animal, male or female, which triggers either the actual mating or an
attack. This behaviour is found amongst most diurnal geckoes. During
the mating the females are held firmly by the male biting them in the
neck. The 5 × 3 mm eggs are usually laid in pairs beneath loose tree
bark. At a temperature of 28 °C the 25 mm young require 45–50 days
to hatch. The eggs are not covered during incubation and should be
kept at an atmospheric humidity of around 75%. The young should be
reared individually in mini-vivaria. Suitable foods for the young are

small waxmoth larvae, minute crickets, fruit flies, banana, and banana-based baby food.

Food: Waxmoth larvae, field crickets, house crickets, fruit flies, banana, and banana-based baby food.

Nactus (Kluge, 1983)

Geckoes of this genus are predominantly ground-dwelling, clawed animals. Earlier these animals were assigned to the genus *Cyrtodactylus*. In Asia they have an enormous distribution range. From a total of 3 species, 2 live in Australia. They are very fast animals which lead a secretive lifestyle.

Nactus arnouxii (Duméril, 1851)

Distribution: Indo-Pacific region, Australia, New Caledonia, New Guinea, Hawaii.

Habitat: Usually on the ground beneath flat rocks and leaf mould and between the roots of trees. In Australia they can also be found on cliff faces. They can only be found in areas of high atmospheric humidity.

Size: 150 mm.

Characteristics: The ground colour is grey-brown to dark brown. According to their origins the animals have several dark brown and light beige spots along the back. Because of the multiplicity of tubercular scales, the upper body has a very rough surface.

Vivarium: Type III. Several hiding places must be provided at ground level. A layer of leaf mould as substrate will be a very close approximation to that found in the natural habitat. Two–three animals require a ground area of at least 0.25 m² and the atmospheric humidity should be around 73%.

Husbandry and reproduction: To date only animals from New Caledonia have reached Europe. This species is parthenogenic. The hard-shelled eggs are hidden on the ground and are very difficult to find. This is because when they are laid the female rolls them in the earth whilst they are still soft. The earth adheres to them, giving them perfect camouflage. Incubation in vermiculite presents no problems.

Food: Crickets, small locusts, springtails, waxmoth larvae.

Similar species: *N. galgajuga* remains somewhat smaller and lives

Nactus arnouxii.

mainly on cliffs in northern Australia. This species also needs high humidity. The males have preanal and femoral pores.

Pachydactylus (Wiegmann, 1834)

This species is endemic to the African continent, and it is in southern Africa where most species are found. They have adapted to all habitats and can thus be found on the ground, on trees, and as a follower of civilisation, also on house walls. They are mainly small geckoes with a total length of 100 mm. Some species remain even smaller, e.g., *P. labialis, P. caraculicus, P. geitje, P. oculatus, P. punctatus, P. scutatus, P. serval,* and *P. sansteyni.* In comparison, the species *P. bibroni* and *P. tetensis,* at around 200 mm, are virtual giants. Most species live in arid to semi-arid regions.

Pachydactylus bibroni (A. Smith, 1846)

Distribution: Southern Africa.
Habitat: These geckoes live amongst rocks, on trees, and in houses. They may therefore be described as followers of civilisation.
Size: 200 mm.
Characteristics: A massive gecko with a wide triangular head. The large granular scales which cover the entire body are very prominent. The tail is segmented and has large, backward-pointing tubercular scales. The colouring is grey-brown to reddish-brown with several irregular white spots.
Vivarium: Type III. The vivarium should be higher than it is wide because these geckoes enjoy climbing the walls and amongst branches. They rarely are on the ground. The vivarium should be sprayed daily.
Husbandry and reproduction: Despite their size these animals are not aggressive towards one another. However, two males may not be kept together without aggression. The males may only be distinguished from the females by their somewhat wider postanal area. When fully grown the males are slightly larger than the females. During mating the females are held firmly in position by a bite to the neck. When oviposition is imminent the female digs a hole in which the eggs are subsequently laid. They can usually be easily found later by the small mound covering the eggs. At a temperature of 28 °C the 55 mm young

Pachydactylus oculatus.

hatch after 45–50 days. Rearing the young on crickets and waxmoth larvae presents no problems.
Food: Field crickets, house crickets, small locusts, moths, waxmoth larvae, springtails, and any other small insects.

Pachydactylus oculatus (Hewitt, 1927)

Distribution: Southern Africa.
Habitat: This species lives on the savannahs of South Africa and prefers a sandy substrate. The animals are usually found beneath rocks, on cliff faces and under the bark of dead trees.
Size: 100 mm.
Characteristics: This is a very attractively coloured gecko. The ground colour is beige to pink, with large dark flecks framed in a lighter colour. The tail is usually slender and elongated. Regenerated tails are

usually turnip-shaped. The scalation is small fine scales interspaced with tubercular scales.

Vivarium: Type II. A suitable substrate is a layer of sand some 2 cm deep. Several flat rocks should be stacked against the rear and side walls. A potted plant and several climbing branches complete the furnishings.

Husbandry and reproduction: This is a small, lively gecko which, despite its nocturnal lifestyle, can often be seen during the day. They are best kept in pairs or in a group of one male with two to three females. They enjoy climbing on branches and during their activity period are constantly scurrying around in the search for food. During the breeding season the female lays 2–3 clutches of two hard-shelled eggs which are buried in the sand. Incubation takes place at 28 °C and requires around 60 days. The young, which measure 30–35 mm, take around 2 years to reach sexual maturity.

Food: Small crickets and locusts, mealworms, waxmoth larvae, and the larvae of grain beetles.

Similar species: *Pachydactylus maculatus, Pachydactylus mariquensis.*

Palmatogecko

Palmatogecko rangei (Anderson, 1908)

Distribution: South Africa (Namib Desert).

Habitat: These geckoes spend the daytime in tunnels which they dig themselves. At night they are very active even when the temperature drops below 10 °C. They get some of their moisture from the local mists and from the resulting dew. The actual habitat of these geckoes is the sand dunes of the Namib Desert.

Size: 140 mm.

Characteristics: This species has thin, almost transparent skin. The upper body is light pink to light brown with irregular dark bands and flecks. The light underside is strongly delineated along the flanks. Characteristic of this species is the skin between the toes, somewhat resembling webbed feet. This prevents their sinking into the loose sand. Males may be recognised by the enlarged hemipenes pockets.

Vivarium: Type I. A section of the vivarium must be kept constantly

Palmatogecko rangei.

moist, whilst another section should have a localised temperature of over 30 °C. A greatly reduced temperature at night is vital. Daily spraying of the vivarium in the early hours of the morning is very beneficial for these creatures.

Husbandry and reproduction: With adequate floor area several pairs may be kept together. For 2–3 pairs a floor area of 0.5 m² is required. These animals are not aggressive towards one another so several males may be kept together. During mating the female is held firmly by a copulation bite. The 14 × 9 mm eggs are buried in the sand so that the sand adheres to them. The eggs should be transferred to an incubator. Care should be taken when removing them because they are extremely thin-shelled. The eggs should not be covered and should be incubated at around 28 °C with an atmospheric humidity of 75%. The young hatch after around 60 days and are easily reared. They should be fed on minute waxmoth larvae, crickets, and locusts. Fruitfly may also be given occasionally. The young are sexually mature after 1 year.

Food: Field crickets, house crickets, small locusts, waxmoth larvae, and other small insects.

Juvenile Paroedura bastardi.

Paroedura (Günther, 1879)

The nine species of the genus *Paroedura* (Dixon & Kroll, 1974) live exclusively in Madagascar and on the Comoros Islands. Most species are ground dwellers but can sometimes also be found on cliffs and the lower reaches of tree trunks. They are extremely beautiful creatures which are especially suitable for life in the vivarium.

Paroedura bastardi (Mocquard, 1900)

Distribution: South and central Madagascar.
Habitat: This species lives in the dry forests and thorn forest region in the south and on the mountain tops of the Massif Central.
Size: 130 mm.
Characteristics: *Paroedura bastardi* has a very compact body and a very large head. The body scales are fine with interspaced tubercular scales especially on the head, back, and tail. In addition the tail is covered in rows of spiny scales. The ground colour is grey to beige or brown with light and dark flecks. The juveniles have two cream-coloured trans-

Paroedura bastardi.

verse bands bordered in brown. As they grow they lose this attractive juvenile pattern.

Vivarium: Type III. A mixture of sand and peat or forest earth provides a suitable substrate, part of which should be kept permanently moist. Several rocks, and pieces of tree bark or cork bark should be placed on the ground to provide adequate hiding places. In addition, several longer pieces of bark should be fitted in an upright position to the rear and side walls of the vivarium.

Husbandry and reproduction: The males are very intolerant of one another, making it possible only to keep pairs or one male with several females. In the wild the breeding season is from September to April, but in the vivarium breeding takes place from April to October. Every 3–4 weeks the female lays two individual hard-shelled eggs which are buried in the moist section of the substrate. At a temperature of 28 °C,

and a relative atmospheric humidity of 80%, the young hatch after 60–70 days. The young grow extremely quickly and are sexually mature at 1 year old.
Food: Field crickets, house crickets, small locusts, small beetles, and waxmoth larvae.

Paroedura pictus (Peters, 1854)

Distribution: South and Southwest Madagascar.
Habitat: This species lives in dry forests, in the thorn bush savannah, and even amongst the sand dunes in the semi-desert regions. In these areas they utilise the most divergent hiding places, e.g., beneath rocks, under loose bark, or simply burrowed into the sand.
Size: 140 mm.
Characteristics: *P. pictus* has a cylindrically shaped body and a conspicuously large head. The scales are small, interspaced with irregular, large tubercular scales. The ground colour consists of various brown tones with light, white to cream-coloured spots. The young are beautifully marked. On a light brown background they have 4–5 white to yellow transverse bands along the back. The tail is also banded. As they grow older they lose this juvenile pattern and by the time they reach adulthood it is only barely discernable.
Vivarium: Type I or II. A suitable substrate is sand, part of which should be kept constantly moist. Loosely stacked flat rocks provide suitable hiding places as do pieces of tree bark and cork bark placed on the ground.
Husbandry and reproduction: This species is best kept in pairs. Whilst in the wild these geckoes breed from September to May, in the vivarium they will breed throughout the year if kept under correct and unvarying conditions. Mating usually takes place late in the evening, the male biting the female on the neck during the process. Three weeks after mating the females lay two hard-shelled, but very thin-shelled eggs. Well-fed animals will lay a clutch of eggs regularly every 3 weeks. At a temperature of 28 °C and a relative atmospheric humidity of 80% they will hatch after 56–60 days. The young grow very quickly and can be sexually mature after only 6–9 months.

Paroedura pictus.

Food: Field crickets, house crickets, small locusts, waxmoth larvae, small beetles, and any other small insects.

Paroedura stumpffi (Boettger, 1879)

Distribution: Known only from the island of Nosy Bé to the northwest of Madagascar.
Habitat: On the ground in the rain forests and overgrown plantations. During the day this species usually sleeps under the bark of old trees.
Size: 130 mm.
Characteristics: *P. stumpffi* has a slender body with a large head. The scales are very small. The ground colour is mainly a brown tone with a light-yellowish to beige pattern. Particularly noticeable is the

Paroedura stumpffi with an egg clearly visible through the skin.

bronze-coloured eye stripe which is present even in newly hatched young.

Vivarium: Type IV. Forest loam with peat and moss provides a suitable substrate. Several pieces of bark or cork should be placed on the ground to provide hiding places. In addition, several pieces of bark should be placed upright on the rear or side walls. Some climbing branches and a bushy potted plant complete the furnishings.

Husbandry and reproduction: This species is best kept in a group of one male with three females. As opposed to other *Paroedura* species, *P. stumpffi* enjoys climbing amongst branches. This species is also remarkable because of its hunting behaviour. They suspend themselves motionlessly, head downwards, until suitable prey passes. The prey is then promptly ambushed and devoured. *P. stumpffi* is also a very fertile species. In the vivarium it will breed continuously from April to October. Every 3–4 weeks the female lays two hard-shelled eggs. At a temperature of 26 °C, and a relative humidity of 80–100%, the young hatch after around 60 days.

Food: Field crickets, house crickets, small locusts, waxmoths and their larvae, springtails, and other small insects and beetles.

Similar species: *P. sanctijohannis, P. homalorhinus, P. gracilis.* Another inhabitant of the rain forest is *P. oviceps* but this species lives on the banks of streams.

Phelsuma (Gray, 1825)

The distribution of this diurnal genus stretches from the east coast of Africa (introduced) through the islands of the Indian Ocean to the Andamans. No *Phelsuma* are found between the 70th and 90th eastern degrees of longitude. The main range of distribution is Madagascar as well as the island groups Seychelles, Mascarenes, and Comoros.

Recently several new species and subspecies have been discovered and described. This is largely due to the efforts of H. Meier of Hamburg. His untiring work with these animals has provided us with much greater knowledge of this genus.

Almost all *Phelsuma* live arboreally. Some smaller species prefer to live on banana trees, some on sugar cane, and some even on garden fences. Only one species spends time on the ground, or beneath rocks lying on the ground. This species is *P. barbouri*.

Many species have adapted to changed habitats. The following species are followers of civilisation: *P. dubia, P. laticauda, P. lineata chloroscelis, P. leiogaster, P. lineata lineata, P. madagascariensis grandis, P. mutabilis, P. quadriocellata*, and *P. sundbergi*.

The most endangered are those species which are governed by limited biotopes (islands) or specialised feeding habits (e.g., rain forest animals). Members of this group are *P. flavigularis, P. guentheri, P. guimbeaui rosagularis, P. guttata, P. madagascariensis boehmei, P. newtonii* (this species is already regarded as being extinct), and *P. seippi*. The degree of threat is often falsely estimated because of the inaccessibility of the various biotopes. Thus species which were thought to be severely endangered have been found elsewhere in large populations, such as *P. standingi*.

Most *Phelsuma* species are very colourful and beautiful creatures. Exceptions are *P. mutabilis, P. modesta*, and *P. guentheri* which have only various brown tones. All other species are more or less green in colour with various red spots and stripes. The sizes range from the smallest *P. pusilla* length of only 80 mm to the largest *P. guentheri* at over 300 mm. The possibility of maintaining rare species in captivity has been attempted by several working groups of interested herpetologists. One of those most dedicated to this cause is G. Hallmann of Dortmund. The species *P. pusilla hallmanni* was named in his honour.

The future of some species is assured because of the large numbers kept and regularly bred by interested and responsible herpetologists. Amongst these are the species *P. madagascariensis madagascariensis, P. madagascariensis grandis*, and *P. standingi*. Many other species are also regularly bred in captivity.

All Phelsumas lay hard-shelled eggs. Only the way in which the eggs are laid is different. Some species hide the eggs on the ground, e.g., *P. seippi* and some populations of *P. standingi*. Other species affix their eggs between dry banana leaves, like *P. dubia*. The majority lay individual or double eggs in a protected hiding place. It often happens that several females lay their eggs in the same place. Immediately after being laid the eggs are held by the hind feet until they have hardened.

Phelsuma pusilla hallmani.

Whilst it is still soft, the second egg is pressed against the first until they adhere together, and in this way the "double clutch" is formed.

The "sticking" species press their eggs against a firm foundation by lying on their back and holding the eggs in their hind feet. All Phelsumas from the Mascarenes affix their eggs to a solid foundation as do *P. flavigularis, P. klemmeri, P. leiogaster, P. dubia*, and *P. barbouri.* All other species lay their eggs without affixing them to a solid foundation. An atmospheric humidity of around 75% is beneficial for the developing young. With 100% humidity it has often been seen that the perfectly formed young die shortly before hatching. The cause of this is probably that when the young split the shell, water penetrates into the egg and the young drown. The young should be reared individually in mini-vivaria and it is vital that sufficient food is always available. All food should be liberally sprinkled with calcium, and a vitamin preparation should be added to the drinking water. Most species may be kept in pairs.

Phelsuma barbouri (Loveridge, 1942)

Distribution: Central Madagascar, Ankarata Massif.
Habitat: A ground-dwelling species which can be found on rocks and in the grassy highlands. At night the climate is cool and misty. During the day there is intense sunshine but the temperature does not rise above 30 °C.
Size: 135 mm.
Characteristics: Several dark brown to black flecks and stripes on a dark green background. A dosolateral line goes along each side of the body from the tip of the snout to the joint of the tail. Below that there is a lateral light green stripe followed by a further dark brown stripe which marks the start of the grey underside.
Vivarium: Type V. It has been observed that these animals enjoy climbing. For this reason the vivarium should contain several stout branches. The females affix their eggs to the underside of flat stacked rocks.
Husbandry and reproduction: This species requires a great variation in the day-night temperature. During the night the temperature should drop to 20 °C or below, but before the temperature is reduced the vi-

Phelsuma barbouri.

varium should be sprayed. Unfortunately, very little is known about this extremely interesting species. They have been bred several times in captivity but to date no useful breeding data is available. The young may be reared in the vivarium and will not be attacked by the adults.
<u>Food</u>: See *P. laticauda*.

Phelsuma cepediana (Merrem, 1820)

<u>Distribution</u>: Mauritius.
<u>Habitat</u>: Regions with heavy rainfall. The highlands of the island of Mauritius, on palm trees, banana trees, and as followers of civilisation, on the walls of houses.
<u>Size</u>: 150 mm. Females remain smaller.
<u>Characteristics</u>: Along the back there are usually pairs of deep red spots which are flanked by a complete or broken dorsolateral stripe of

Phelsuma cepediana.

the same colour. The ground colour goes from light green to turquoise-blue. The males may be recognised by their prominent preanal pores.
Vivarium: Type II. The vivarium should be densely planted. Some thick bamboo poles should also be provided. The lighting should be bright. Temperature during the day up to 30 °C and at night not below 20 °C. High atmospheric humidity is vital, and the vivarium should be sprayed daily.
Husbandry and reproduction: This species may only be kept in pairs. These animals are very unsociable, even towards other Phelsumas. During courtship the males display their most beautiful colours. With jerky movements, head-bobbing, and tongue flicking, the male ap-

proaches the female. If she is ready to mate the male is allowed to approach from the rear. He holds the female in position with a bite to the neck, and copulation takes place. Several hiding places should be provided and it is here that the female will lay her eggs. Short pieces of bamboo, open at one end, are suitable and are especially favoured places for the laying of eggs. At a temperature of 28 °C the 40 mm young take 40–45 days to hatch. They are somewhat delicate and require an atmospheric humidity of 75%.

Food: Waxmoth larvae, small crickets, small locusts, fruitfly, house flies, sweet fruit, and fruit-based baby food.

Phelsuma guttata (Kaudern, 1922)

Distribution: Eastern Madagascar, Sainte Marie, Nosy Mangabe.
Habitat: A purely arboreal forest *Phelsuma* only to be found in continuous rain forest regions.
Size: 130 mm.
Characteristics: A slender gecko with a sharply pointed head. The ground colour is dark green with dark lines running along the flanks. A dark line runs from the snout to behind the eye. On the extremities there are light spots enclosed in dark brown. Along the back there can be dark brown to bright red spots and in the neck region several V-shaped stripes. Some populations have blue colouring in the neck region.
Vivarium: Type IV. For their well-being these animals require a densely planted rain forest vivarium containing several stout branches and some thick bamboo poles.
Husbandry and reproduction: In a well planted vivarium, one male may be kept with several females. The vivarium must be sprayed daily. A temperature of 20–25 °C is quite adequate. This species does not tolerate direct sunlight. Mating is carried out in the same way as other Phelsumas. Here too the male uses a copulation bite to hold the female in position. The eggs are hidden on the ground beneath leaf mould or bark. They are usually double-eggs measuring 11 × 8 mm. At a temperature of 28 °C the 45 mm young hatch after 40–45 days. To rear the young successfully, high atmospheric humidity is required, and they

Phelsuma guttata.

should be reared individually in small vivaria. The young are sexually mature after only 10–12 months. Males may be recognised by the prominent hemipenes pockets. Moreover, they have easily visible preanofemoral pores.

Food: See *Phelsuma laticauda*.

Phelsuma klemmeri (Seipp, 1991)

Distribution: Northwest Madagascar.
Habitat: Regions with pronounced rainy and dry seasons. At the edges of forests and bamboo groves.
Size: 90 mm.

Phelsuma klemmeri.

Characteristics: A conspicuously slender creature with very fine scalation. The extremely pointed head, which is bright yellow, is well set-off from the turquoise-colored body. The somewhat flattened body is similar to that of *P. barbouri*. Males may be recognised by the well-developed preanofemoral pores.

Vivarium: Type III. Dense planting is essential. Finger-thick branches and bamboo poles should be fitted vertically and horizontally in the vivarium. The bamboo should have access holes on the sides.

Husbandry and reproduction: In a vivarium of 40 × 30 × 50 cm (L × W × H) one male may be kept with two females. So that all animals are fully active, a localised temperature of 35 °C is vital. This may be achieved by means of a spotlight which is in operation for 2–3 hours. It is only in full sunlight when these geckoes display their full beauty. The mating behaviour is similar to that of other Phelsumas. Here again the female is held in position by a bite to the neck. The females lay their 6 mm eggs, usually double-eggs, inside the bamboo poles.

Food: Only the most minute food should be given. Fruitfly, small ermine moths and their larvae, waxmoth larvae, hatchling crickets, banana, and banana-based baby food.

Phelsuma laticauda (Boettger, 1880)

Distribution: Northwest Madagascar, Nosy Bé and the Comoros Islands.
Habitat: Can frequently be found amongst human habitation. Also on banana plants, trees, and other large plants.
Size: 130 mm.
Characteristics: These animals have a wide, somewhat flattened tail. On the back they have three elongated red spots. The entire neck region is covered in small gold spots. The dark eyes are ringed in turquoise-blue. The blue colour variant is extremely rare.
Vivarium: Type III. Like most Phelsumas, *P. laticauda* requires a great deal of direct sunlight. A spotlight should be used to achieve a localised temperature of 35 °C. A vivarium of 40 × 40 × 60 cm (L × W × H) is suitable for one pair of this species. The furnishings consist of several smooth branches or bamboo poles between which some sturdy plants such as Sanseveria should be placed. There should also be adequate ventilation. At night the temperature may safely be reduced to 20 °C. For egg laying, bamboo poles with an open end should be provided. These poles should be of a diameter large enough to allow the female to move around comfortably inside.
Husbandry and reproduction: Only in a very bright light will these animals show their magnificent colours. A few hours sunlight are optimal but beware of overheating. The vivarium should be sprayed every 2–3 days. Water which has been enriched with vitamins will be taken from a drinking pad. Food should be liberally sprinkled with calcium, and once each week powdered calcium should be provided at a dry place in the vivarium. Females will store excess calcium in the calcium sacs behind the head. It has been proved that this species mates immediately after eggs have been laid. This is also the case with other Phelsumas. If an actual mating does not take place, a courtship, which soon ends, is carried out by both sexes.

The females lay their eggs in a suitably protected hiding place (bamboo poles). They are usually double-eggs which are held by the

Phelsuma laticauda, normal colouring and blue variant.

hind feet until they harden. *P. laticauda* does not affix its eggs to a solid foundation. If this does happen then the eggs are invariably infertile or the animals are suffering from a shortage of calcium. In these cases the eggs are usually eaten immediately. At 28 °C the 40 mm young hatch after 4–45 days. Frequently the second young hatches 1 day later. The young should be reared individually in small vivaria. Vitaminised water and calcium-fortified food are vital for the well-being of the young. With good feeding the juveniles are sexually mature in 10–12 months.

Food: Waxmoths, waxmoth larvae, small crickets, house flies, fruitfly, sweet fruit, and fruit-based baby food. Well-fed animals may occasionally be given a 1-week fast.

Phelsuma leiogaster.

Phelsuma leiogaster (Mertens, 1973)

Distribution: Southwest Madagascar.
Habitat: A tree-dwelling species which, as a follower of civilisation, can frequently be found amongst human habitation. It occurs in mainly dry areas.
Size: 130 mm.
Characteristics: The colours consist of muted pastel shades. On a grey-brown background there are reddish-brown stripes from the head to the tip of the tail. A greyish-brown stripe running from behind the eye to the tail delimits the light underside. A colourful sexual dimorphism appears to be present in most animals; the females are thus always a greyish-brown colour.

Vivarium: Type II. For climbing, several finger-thick bamboo poles should be installed vertically in the vivarium. Atmospheric humidity should be kept low (below 50%). Because these animals require a great deal of heat and light to show their full beauty, a spotlight should also be fitted in the vivarium. In the area of the spotlight the temperature should rise to around 35 °C. Fit all energy sources outside the vivarium! There must also be cooler places available in the vivarium.
Husbandry and reproduction: *P. leiogaster* is a species which is very easy to keep. However, because of its somewhat muted colouration, it is not a very popular species amongst *Phelsuma* enthusiasts. The incubation of the eggs should be carried out in the same way as those of *P. laticauda*.
Food: See *Phelsuma laticauda*.

Phelsuma lineata lineata (Gray, 1842)

Distribution: Madagascar (Antananarivo).
Habitat: On trees and on the walls of houses and other buildings.
Size: 120 mm.
Characteristics: On a dark background these geckoes have numerous small red spots scattered over the entire upper body. A black stripe separates the green upper side from the white underside. *P. lineata lineata* is frequently confused with the subspecies *P. l. chloroscelis*. At 145 mm the subspecies is somewhat larger than the nominate form and is known from the Perinet region. Along the back these animals have a large red patch which at the front is strongly delineated and towards the tail turns into two small spots. Between the dark lateral stripes and the underside there is an additional yellow stripe. From Perinet to the east coast of Madagascar the animals become smaller (120 mm) and the colours paler. Even the yellow stripe is not so obvious on animals from the coast. In this case it is probably an individual form which is quite different from the nominate form.
Vivarium: Type III. The furnishings should be the same as those described for *P. laticauda*. A temperature of 25–30 °C is quite adequate. A nightly reduction to 10 °C is not uncommon in the areas around Antananarivo and Perinet during July and August. This should also be taken into account in the husbandry of these animals. For the subspe-

Left: Phelsuma lineata lineata.
Right: Phelsuma lineata chloroscelis.

cies *P. l. chloroscelis* from Perinet an atmospheric humidity of 75%
should be maintained.
Husbandry and reproduction: Males may be recognised by the prominent preanal pores and the enlarged hemipenes pockets. When fully
adult, the males are somewhat larger than the females. This species
also prefers to lay its eggs in hollow bamboo poles. There can be up to
six clutches of eggs each breeding season, each clutch usually containing two eggs. The incubation of the eggs and rearing of the young are
the same as described for *P. laticauda*.
Food: See *Phelsuma laticauda*.

Phelsuma madagascariensis boehmi.

Phelsuma madagascariensis boehmi (Meier, 1982)

Distribution: Eastern Madagascar, Perinet, Ranomafana.
Habitat: A rain forest *Phelsuma* which leads a purely arboreal lifestyle.
Size: 220 mm.
Characteristics: This species is dark green in colour with black skin between the scales. Patterning as in the nominate form.
Vivarium: Type IV. In the wild these animals spend most of their time at the top of trees. The vivarium should therefore be at least 80 cm high. Bamboo poles some 10 cm in diameter have proved to be best for this species.

Husbandry and reproduction: See *P. m. madagascariensis*. During the
months November to January the temperature should be 25–30 °C.
During July and August it should drop to 15 °C at night and rise to
25 °C during the day. This corresponds to their normal temperature
cycle. At 28 °C the young hatch after 48–55 days measuring some 60–65
mm. Incubation and rearing of the young should be carried out in the
same way as described for *P. m. madagascariensis*.
Food: See *P. m. madagascariensis*.

Phelsuma madagascariensis grandis (Gray, 1870)

Distribution: Northern Madagascar, Nosy Bé.
Habitat: Predominantly on trees but also found on banana palms and
houses.
Size: 280 mm. Some individuals may even reach 300 mm.
Characteristics: The ground colour is a vivid green. There is always a
red stripe from each nostril to each eye. Along the back there are red
flecks which may run together to form a barred or wavelike pattern.
The red patterning is variable and in some cases may even be absent.
This is not determined geographically. Animals which have blue spots
in addition to the red flecks are extremely rare. Males are easily distinguished by the well-developed, yellowish preanal pores.
Vivarium: Type III. Upright bamboo poles and very thick branches
should be installed in the vivarium. Some of the bamboo poles should
be hollow to a depth of at least 15 cm and should be accessible to the
animals. Large Sansiverias are extremely suitable plants for this species and will frequently be used for climbing and resting.
Husbandry and reproduction: These geckoes may only be kept in pairs.
The pair should be of equal size because the male may become extremely aggressive during mating. A female less than one year old
should not be allowed to breed. The courtship behaviour of the male is
similar to the threat posture shown to other males. Whether bites are
inflicted depends largely on the behaviour of the female. Mating always takes place immediately after eggs have been laid. The male holds
the female in position by a bite to the neck. Harmonious pairs should
never be separated. The female often suffers injuries if the pair are

Phelsuma madagascariensis grandis.

separated, even for a short time, and then placed together again. In
such cases, females which are not ready to mate immediately will be
attacked as if they were males. The breeding season lasts from September until May, during which time the female will lay one or two eggs
every 4–6 weeks. The eggs are held by the hind feet until they harden.
The female will often do this whilst lying on her back pressing the eggs
against a solid surface. Thick, hollow bamboo poles are ideally suited
to this purpose. Eggs should be incubated at around 28 °C and with
humidity around 75% they will hatch after 60–65 days. The young
measure 67–70 mm on hatching and should be reared individually in
small vivaria. In these small vivaria, high humidity is neccessary. Calcium is also vital.
Food: See *P. m. madagascariensis*

Phelsuma madagascariensis madagascariensis (Gray, 1831)

Distribution: Eastern Madagascar, Sainte Marie.
Habitat: Trees and house walls. Frequently at the edges of forests but
rarely in the forest itself.
Size: 220 mm.
Characteristics: The ground colour is light green to grass-green with
light coloured skin between the scales. Along the back there are reddish-brown to red patches which can sometimes form a dorsal stripe.
There are almost always spots on the top of the head. A wide reddish-
brown stripe runs from the nostril, through the eye and down to the
temporal area.
Vivarium: Type III. Daily spraying is necessary. Bamboo poles 10 cm
in diameter and with an open end should be installed. It is here that
the females will lay their eggs. Temperature 25–28 °C.
Husbandry and reproduction: These geckoes should be housed in a
spacious vivarium which is well planted and contains several hiding
places. Males may be extremely aggressive towards females that are
not ready to mate. If there are insufficient hiding places the females
may suffer severe injury. It is a peculiarity of this species that even a
pair will not always live in harmony. Should this be the case an alternative mate must be found. The mating season begins in November or

Phelsuma m. madagascariensis.

December and continues until March or April. During this time the female may lay up to six clutches consisting of single or double-eggs. They are usually laid inside one of the hiding places (bamboo poles). The eggs should be hatched in a incubator at 28 °C. Incubation takes around 50–55 days and the young emerge measuring around 55–58 mm. The young should be reared individually in small vivaria. High atmospheric humidity is essential. Plants are also vital as is a varied diet liberally sprinkled with calcium.

Food: Waxmoth larvae, crickets, small locusts, flies, springtails and other small insects, banana and banana-based baby food.

Phelsuma quadriocellata (Peters, 1883)

Distribution: Eastern Madagascar, Perinet.
Habitat: Mainly on banana plants but also occasionally on houses.
Size: 120 mm.

Phelsuma quadriocellata.

Characteristics: The upper body is green with red spots and stripes along the back. Characteristic of this species are the blue eye spots immediately behind the forelegs. These spots are outlined in light to turquoise-blue. The dark eyes are outlined in yellow and on the head and neck area there are small blue spots. The tail is somewhat flattened.

Vivarium: Type III. The vivarium should contain some thick bamboo poles and several broad-leaved bushy plants. Some of the bamboo poles should have an open end, allowing the females access to lay their eggs.

During the day the temperature should be 28–30 °C, dropping to 20 °C at night. During the day the humidity should be 75% whilst at night it should be increased to 90–100%. In the wild, the temperature in their natural habitat is 10 °C at night during July and August, and during ʾhe day reaches a maximum of 25 °C. This should be taken into ac- ʾ in captivity.

ʾʾy and reproduction: When keeping this demanding species it that approximate natural conditions are maintained. Ani- ʾons with pronounced climatic variations are always moɾᴜ ʾcal. One pair may be kept in a vivarium measuring 40 × 30 ᴜᴜ ᴜᴜ (ᴸ × W × H). During the breeding season the females lay double-eggs every 3–5 weeks. Very rarely they lay only one egg. A total of six clutches, rarely more, will be produced each season. The eggs are laid in hollow bamboo poles or at the joint of a leaf to a plant stem. With a temperature of 28 °C and atmospheric humidity at 75% the 30 mm young will hatch after 40–45 days. They should be reared individually in small vivaria (see *P. laticauda*).
Food: See *P. laticauda*.

Phelsuma seippi (Meier, 1987)

Distribution: Madagascar, Nosy Bé.
Habitat: A purely arboreal species which lives in and at the edges of forests.
Size: 140 mm.
Characteristics: The pointed snout, on which a reddish-brown to dark brown stripe runs through the eye to above the ear, is particularly no- ticeable. The upper body is green with several red to reddish-brown spots. The red stripe along the back is not always present. On the light underside of the head there are several V-shaped markings. The under- side of the body is light pink.
Vivarium: Type IV. Dense planting with finger to arm-thick branches. Frequent spraying is vital.
Husbandry and reproduction: See *P. guttata*. This species also hides its eggs on the ground under leaf mould. At a temperature of 28 °C the 38–40 mm young take 45–50 days to hatch.
Food: See *P. laticauda*.

Phelsuma seippi.

Phelsuma serraticauda (Mertens, 1963)

Distribution: Eastern Madagascar, north of Tamatave.
Habitat: Usually on coconut palms, rarely on banana plants.
Size: 130 mm.
Characteristics: The ground colour varies from dark green to yel-
lowish-green. There are three red transverse bands on the head and
three more brightly coloured longitudinal stripes on the back near the
tail joint. At the actual tail joint there are numerous red spots. Typical
of this species is the dorsoventrally flattened, saw-shaped tail. The
throat is bright yellow.
Vivarium: See *P. laticauda*.
Husbandry and reproduction: This species lives high in the crowns of
coconut palms. Here one finds groups of one male with 3–5 females.
This type of grouping is only possible in large, spacious vivaria. Even
amongst the females there is a seniority system, so that sufficient
hiding places should be provided. During the breeding season, from

Phelsuma serraticauda.

December–March, a female will lay up to four clutches of eggs, usually double-eggs, and only rarely single. At a temperature of 28 °C and an atmospheric humidity of 75% the 40 mm young take 53–58 days to hatch. The second egg usually hatches one day after the first. The young should be reared individually in small vivaria. The young are extremely aggressive towards other geckoes and even towards members of their own species. When they are given sufficient calcium and their drinking water is regularly vitaminised, rearing presents no problems.

Food: See *P. laticauda.*

Ptychozoon (Kuhl, 1822)

There are five known species of the genus *Ptychozoon*. They are all found in southeast Asia and are all rain forest dwellers with a prominent fold of skin along each side of the body. This has given them their common name "Flying Gecko".

Ptychozoon lionotum (Annandale, 1905)

Distribution: Southern Burma, Thailand, and on the island of Ramri.
Habitat: Flying Geckoes are exclusively rain forest animals which spend the day beneath loose tree bark. Because of their excellent camouflage it is almost impossible to see them when resting on trees.
Size: 165 mm.
Characteristics: The body and tail are quite flattened. The scales are fine, making this animal feel like velvet to the touch. The most obvious characteristic of this species is the folds of skin along each side of the body. In this species the fold of skin begins at the side of the head and reaches to the tip of the tail. It is only broken at the neck area. They also have folds of skin on the sides of the hind legs and on the lower sections of the forelegs. The ground colour is a brownish-grey with large whitish flecks and some smaller dark flecks. In addition there are wave-shaped transverse bands across the body. In the past, *P. lionotum* was frequently confused with *P. kuhli*. They are best distinguished by the original tail. In the case of *P. lionotum* the loose skin on the sides of the tail is serrated to the tip and the tail gradually becomes thinner, whilst the loose skin at the end of the tail of *P. kuhli* becomes much wider and is not serrated.
Vivarium: Type IV. A suitable substrate is a layer of clay balls used in hydroponic plant culture covered by moss or leaf mould. The rear and side walls should be covered with cork tiles. These will be the favourite resting places of these geckoes. Stout branches should be provided for climbing, as should some hollow bamboo poles as hiding places. Dense planting completes the furnishing of the vivarium.
Husbandry and reproduction: This is a very sociable species which is best kept in small groups. The temperature should be around 28 °C during the day with a nightly reduction of around 5 °C. The atmospheric humidity should always be 80–100%. Under these constant conditions this species will breed throughout the year. The female lays two

Ptychozoon kuhli.

hard-shelled eggs, usually as "double-eggs" which she affixes to a solid foundation in a protected place. Hatching takes 65–70 days at a temperature of 25–30 °C and a relative atmospheric humidity above 80%. The 52–55 mm young should be reared individually and will reach sexual maturity after around 1 year.

Food: Waxmoths, waxmoth larvae, crickets, springtails, and other small insects.

Similar species: *P. horsfieldii*, *P. intermedium*, and *P. kuhli* may be kept under the same conditions. It is only *P. rhacophorus* which requires somewhat lower temperatures.

Ptyodactylus (Goldfuss, 1820)

The fan-like feet of this species have given rise to its common name "Fan-Fingered Gecko". Its distribution range is the north of Africa from Cameroon through the Arabian Peninsula to Pakistan. Here they live on cliffs and rocks in the desert regions. Because the temperatures drop dramatically at night this species is often very active during the day. They attempt to reach their preferred temperature during the early morning and early evening.

Ptyodactylus ragazzi (Anderson, 1898)

Distribution: From Mali to Ethiopia.
Habitat: Lives on cliffs and rocks in desert regions.
Size: 160 mm.
Characteristics: A robust species with a stout body. In most animals the tail is regenerated. There is a reticulated pattern on a beige background.
Vivarium: Type II. The vivarium should have a rock-clad rear wall containing several hiding places. The dimensions of the ground area are unimportant. A spot which has a localised temperature of 30 °C during the day will frequently be sought out by these animals. This temperature is achieved by means of a spotlight. To prevent burns the animals must not be able to touch the spotlight.
Husbandry and reproduction: Only one male and one female may be kept together. The males may be recognised by their prominent hemipenes pockets. Males are very aggressive towards one another. This species has been bred several times in captivity. The females lay their eggs in rock crevices where they are affixed to a solid foundation. At a room temperature of 18–20 °C the 55 mm young take more than 100 days to hatch. When sufficient food is provided the young may be reared with the adults. Shortly before the eggs are laid the females are very susceptible to stress and must not be disturbed unneccessarily. Whilst gravid the females will eat an increased amount of calcium.
Food: Crickets, waxmoths, waxmoth larvae.
Similar species: All Ptyodactylus species have a similar lifestyle. At 120 mm, P. oudrii is the smallest species. Keeping one male with several females presents no problems.

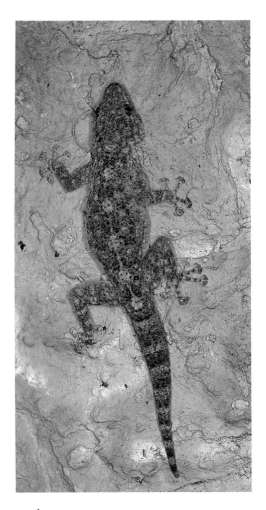

Ptyodactylus ragazzi.

Saurodactylus (Fitzinger, 1843)

This genus with the species *S. fasciatus, S. mauritanicus*, and the subspecies *S. m. brosseti* is known only from Morocco. Whilst the species *S. m. mauritanicus* occurs along the coast, the subspecies *S. m. brosseti* and the species *S. fasciatus* are found inland up to an altitude of 1000 m. The daylight hours are spent below flat rocks lying on the ground, or amongst piles of boulders. When they are first uncovered they lie still for a moment and then flee at great speed to seek protection beneath another rock. They are fully grown at a length of 60 mm and have no clinging lamellae.

Saurodactylus mauritanicus brosseti (Bons & Pasteur, 1957)

Distribution: North Africa, southwest Morocco.
Habitat: Can be found on grassy slopes as well as amongst rocks and piles of boulders.
Size: 60 mm.
Characteristics: Along the back these animals are dark brown with yellow spots. These can also form a yellow band running from the snout through the eye to the neck on top of the head. The tail is yellow to orange interrupted by dark brown spots and stripes.
Vivarium: Type I. The entire vivarium must be kept dry. The geckoes drink from a shallow water container and should be sprayed every second evening. A localised ground temperature of 28 °C will be regularly sought out during the day.
Husbandry and reproduction: A group of one male and three females may be kept together without any problems in a vivarium with a ground area of 0.2 m². The height is unimportant because these geckoes are exclusively ground-dwellers. From May until September the females will lay their single egg 1 cm deep in the sandy substrate. It is always a single, hard-shelled, spherical egg of 5 mm diameter. This occurs in a 4-week cycle. At a temperature of 25–28 °C the 20–30 mm young take 55–60 days to hatch. The young are dark brown to black without the spotted pattern. The tail is bright yellow to orange-yellow. The young should be reared individually in small vivaria and should be fed on springtails, small waxmoth larvae, hatchling crickets, and wingless fruitfly. All food should be liberally sprinkled with calcium.
Food: Waxmoth larvae, hatchling crickets, wingless fruitfly, and other small insects.

Stenodactylus (Fitzinger, 1826)

This genus is distributed from northern Africa to Asia Minor. They are ground dwellers which can be found in deserts and semi-deserts. The

Saurodactylus mauritanicus brosseti.

comb-like fringes on the toes prevent the geckoes from sinking into the loose sand.

Stenodactylus sthenodactylus (Lichtenstein, 1823)

Distribution: Northern Africa and southwest Asia.
Habitat: Dry, stony semi-deserts. During the day below rocks and wood.
Size: 100 mm.
Characteristics: These animals vary between shades of brown with dark spots. Some of the dark spots can run together, forming a reticulated pattern.
Vivarium: Type I. All hiding places on the floor of the vivarium should be firmly fixed to prevent the animal burrowing below them. There should be localised ground temperature of 30 °C. The vivarium should be given a light spray each evening.
Husbandry and reproduction: One male may be kept with several females. The males will not inflict injuries on one another but the dominant male will suppress all others in the vivarium. In December or January these geckoes should be given a 4–6 week hibernation period

Stenodactylus sthenodactylus.

at temperatures below 20 °C. This will have a stimulating effect on subsequent mating. During courtship the male approaches the female waving his tail. The male may also emit a shrill whistle. After following the female for some time the male takes the female and holds her in position by a bite to the neck. Copulation lasts up to 30 seconds. In most cases the eggs are buried; only rarely are they left lying on the surface of the substrate. For this reason the substrate should be a layer of sand several centimetres deep. To be able to check them more easily, the eggs should be hatched in an incubator. At 28 °C the 30–35 mm young hatch after 75–80 days. Rearing them on small waxmoth larvae, fruitfly, and small springtails presents no problems.
Food: Small crickets, waxmoth larvae, wingless fruitfly, springtails, and other small insects.

Tarentola (Gray, 1825)

This genus consists of 14 species which can be found in the Mediterranean region, North Africa, on the Canary Islands, and in the southern United States. Some species have developed as followers of civilisation.

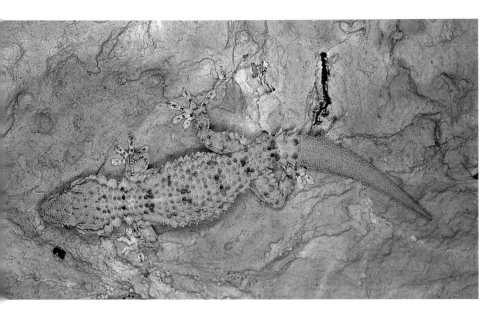

Tarentola mauritanica.

These animals are usually active at twilight, although during periods of bad weather they can also be seen basking during the day.

Tarentola mauritanica (Linnaeus, 1758)

Distribution: Mediterranean region and North Africa.
Habitat: Cliff faces, beneath bank, on dry stone walls, on houses.
Size: 160 mm.
Characteristics: The Moorish Gecko has a strong body. The most noticeable feature is the keeled tubercular scalation along the back. These are arranged in both transverse and longitudinal rows. The colouring goes from grey to dark brown, but most animals have a light-dark marbled pattern. Juveniles have wave-shaped, serrated transverse bands along the back.
Vivarium: Type II. The substrate should be a layer of sand 3 cm deep. There should be several stacks of flat rocks as well as some flat rocks standing upright. A potted plant completes the arrangement.
Husbandry and reproduction: Because of the very aggressive defence of its territory, the Moorish Gecko is very unsociable and may only be

kept in individual pairs. A pronounced annual cycle is essential for successful breeding. During hibernation the temperature should be around 15–20 °C, whilst during the activity period it should be around 28–30 °C. A nightly reduction of 5–6 °C is also vital. The breeding season stretches from April to August and during this time the female will lay 4–6 clutches of 2 hard-shelled eggs at intervals of around 3 weeks. The eggs will normally be laid in a slightly moist position, but they must be incubated under perfectly dry conditions. At 26–30 °C the young will hatch after around 70 days. Because this species is extremely cannibalistic the young must be reared separately. Aggression has not been observed amongst the juveniles so they may be reared together or alongside other species. The young will become sexually mature in 1–2 years.

Food: Crickets, small locusts, beetles, springtails, waxmoths and their larvae, and other small insects.

Similar species: All other *Tarentola* species.

Teratoscincus (Strauch, 1863)

The geckoes of this genus are purely terrestrial animals found in the semi-arid to arid regions of southwest and central Asia. They live in burrows up to 80 cm deep which they excavate themselves; at this depth there is always a certain degree of moisture. This is also known from other desert dwellers (see *Nephrurus*). The scales of all species are arranged like roof tiles and are very easily dislodged (see Skin and Scalation). As is the case with other desert dwellers they have a sort of "winking scale" above the eye. This is an adaptation to their natural habitat. In addition these animals have saw-like scalation on the toes which enables them to move quickly over fine sand. With a total length of 200 mm *T. keyzerlingii* is the largest gecko of this genus. Not only the size and appearance of this subspecies indicate that it should be a separate species, but also the fact that it will not interbreed with the nominate species.

Teratoscincus scincus (Schlegel, 1858)

Distribution: Southwest and central Asia, northern Afghanistan, northern Iran, northwest Pakistan, southern Russia to western China.

Habitat: This species lives amongst sand dunes with sparse vegetation,

Teratoscincus scincus.

mainly in desert regions with considerable temperature variations; over 40 °C during the day, dropping to 20 °C at night.

Size: 170 mm.

Characteristics: The ground colour is greyish-yellow to yellowish-pink with dark brown to black spots and stripes. On the upper side of the tail there are large overlapping scales.

Vivarium: Type I. A ground area of 0.2 m² is sufficient for one pair. One part of the vivarium should have a layer of sand at least 10 cm deep, the lower reaches of which should be kept permanently moist. This is achieved by inserting a vertical tube into which a little water is poured each day. The ground heating should be in operation for 2–3 hours after the lights have been switched off. This enables the animals to reach their desired temperature. Here the localised ground temperature may safely reach 30 °C. For the remainder of the night the temperature should sink to 20–22 °C.

Husbandry and reproduction: Because these animals are accustomed to a hibernation period in the wild this should be taken into consideration when keeping them in captivity. A 3–4 week rest period with reduced lighting and temperatures of 10–15 °C increases the desire to mate. During the year the female will lay two to three clutches of eggs. They are very thin-walled, hard-shelled eggs which are extremely fragile. They are usually buried several centimetres deep in a warm and dry position in the vivarium. It is advisable to hatch the eggs in an incubator. Great care must be taken when removing the eggs from the vivarium to the incubator. They should be uncovered using a fine paint brush and should be removed on a small spoon. The clutch should be incubated under completely dry conditions at a temperature of 28–32 °C. After 75–95 days the young will hatch measuring around 60 mm. Young which hatch in the vivarium will be eaten by the adults. Only a few days after hatching the young will already show the typical and imposing warning behaviour. To do this they stretch up on all fours and wave the tail horizontally. This causes the overlapping scales on the tail to rub against one another creating a chirping or rattling sound, after which the gecko springs towards its aggressor, hissing, squeaking, and biting. It will then retreat rapidly to its burrow. This behaviour is less pronounced in the females. Males may be recognised by their enlarged hemipenes pockets and the easily visible femoral pores.

Food: Crickets, small locusts, springtails, mealworms, waxmoths, waxmoth larvae, beetles, and other small insects. Some adults will also eat pink mice.

Similar species: *T. keyzerlingii, T. microlepis*. Very little is known about the species *T. bedriagai* and *T. przewalskii*. Because all species occur in the same habitats it would be wise to keep them under the same conditions as those described for *T. scincus*. Under these conditions *T. keyzerlingii* and *T. microlepis* have been bred several times in captivity.

Thecadactylus (Goldfuss, 1820)

Thecadactylus rapicauda (Houttuyn, 1782)

Distribution: Central America, northern South America, Caribbean Islands, Trinidad, Tobago, Curacao, Los Testigas, Bonaire, Aruba.

Thecadactylus rapicauda.

Habitat: On trees in the tropical rain forests. Sometimes also on house walls.

Size: There are animals of varying sizes. Those from the Caribbean Islands can reach over 200 mm whilst animals from South America reach only around 150 mm.

Characteristics: The ground colour can vary between yellowish-brown to chocolate brown. Several dark brown to black spots and stripes give these creatures a bark-like appearance. The toes have well developed clinging lamellae which are divided in the centre. Apart from the first toe, all others have a strong retractile claw. The tail is slightly flattened and regenerated tails tend to be turnip-shaped. The velvet-like skin is very easily dislodged.

Vivarium: Type IV. Hollow, upright cork tubes provide the neccessary hiding places.
Husbandry and reproduction: These animals are very slow in their movements. When threatened they arch their back, cat-style, and open the mouth to reveal the blue tongue. After this they inflict a powerful and painful bite. Males may be recognised by the enlarged hemipenes pockets and they are usually smaller than the females. The almost spherical eggs are buried in the substrate. The sizes of the eggs and young differ according to the origin of the parents. With adequate feeding the young may be reared alongside the adults.
Food: Crickets, small locusts, waxmoths, waxmoth larvae, moths, and other small insects.

Tropiocolotes (Peters, 1880)

The genus *Tropiocolotes* consists of four species which are all at home in North Africa and southwest Asia. They live mainly in dry sandy regions.

Tropiocolotes tripolitanus (Peters, 1880)

Distribution: North Africa.
Habitat: This species lives amongst the sand dunes where there is only very sparse vegetation. It is also found on cliffs and in other rocky areas. The daylight hours are usually spent below rocks.
Size: 100 mm.
Characteristics: *Tropiocolotes tripolitanus* is a small terrestrial species the scalation of which consists of large tubercular scales. The ground colour is usually yellowish with scattered dark spots. The tail has dark transverse rings, becoming wider towards the middle. The lower half of the tail is completely dark. The irregular stripe on the head is particularly noticeable. It begins at the tip of the snout, runs through the eyes and ends behind the forelegs.
Vivarium: Type I. The substrate should be a 1–3 cm layer of sand upon which flat rocks and pieces of cork bark are placed.
Husbandry and reproduction: This is a very sociable species which is best kept in small groups. The breeding season stretches from May to October. During this time the females lay up to six clutches of eggs

Tropiocolotes tripolitanus.

at approximately 4-week intervals. Each clutch consists of one hard-shelled egg. For incubation they may be left in the vivarium or transferred to an incubator with a temperature of 25–28 °C. The young hatch after 58–64 days and should be reared separately in small vivaria. A short winter rest period will have a stimulating effect on future mating.

Food: Small field crickets, house crickets, waxmoth larvae, grain beetles, and other small insects.

Similar species: All other *Tropiocolotes* species.

Uroplatus (A. Duméril, 1805)

It is only fairly recently that this genus has been more carefully examined, and it has been shown that many questions still remain unanswered. It has not yet been explained why certain populations of this genus have differently shaped tails although they all occur in the same habitat. All species live in areas of high rainfall. Although the species *U. fimbriatus, U. henkeli, U. sikorae*, and the subspecies *U. s. sameiti* lead a purely arboreal lifestyle, the species *U. alluaudi, U. ebenaui, U. guentheri* and *U. phantasticus* prefer to live amongst bushes. *U. lineatus* holds a special position. If one believes the Madagascans and takes the colouring into consideration, this species prefers the bamboo forests. All species either hide their eggs on the ground or bury them. The males of all species may be recognised by their enlarged hemipenes pockets.

Uroplatus ebenaui (Boettger, 1878)

Distribution: Northern Madagascar and the island of Nosy Bé.
Habitat: On bushes in the rain forest regions. They do not hide during the day. They prefer a range of up to one metre above ground level.
Size: 75 mm.
Characteristics: *U. ebenaui* is the smallest species of this genus. The triangular head, which is well set-off from the body, is particularly noticeable. The similarity to *U. phantasticus* is so pronounced that they may only be distinguished by the difference in tail shape. Whilst *U. ebenaui* has a very short, flat tail serrated at the edges, *U. phantasticus* has a long, flat tail somewhat reminiscent of a leaf. The ground colour can vary from yellowish-brown to dark brown. The rear of the head is usually somewhat darker. There is frequently a vertebral stripe. There are several pointed scales above the eyes, at the rear of the head, along the spine, and on the elbows of the extremities.
Vivarium: Type IV. The vivarium must contain thin climbing branches.
Husbandry and reproduction: Because they are not aggressive towards one another, several pairs may be kept together provided there is sufficient space and enough bushy plants. The almost spherical eggs, which are around 5 mm in diameter and are hard-shelled, are buried in the substrate. They are best incubated in moist vermiculite. Care should be taken that the substrate does not become too dry. At 28 °C the young hatch after 60–70 days and should be fed on waxmoth larvae, small crickets, and other small insects. The atmospheric humidity should not be below 75%.
Food: Small waxmoth larvae, field crickets, house crickets, small locusts, wingless fruitfly.

Uroplatus guentheri (Mocquard, 1908)

Distribution: Northwest Madagascar.
Habitat: This species lives in bushes and on low trees. They prefer to live 1.5–3 m above ground level.
Size: 150 mm.

Uroplatus ebenaui with a juvenile.

Characteristics: These geckoes are a greyish-brown to yellowish-brown in colour. There is a vertebral stripe from the rear of the head to the tip of the tail. There may also be irregular dark brown transverse stripes. The original tail ends in two curves with a central protruding point. This gecko has a unique method of escape; in danger it leaps from the branch, rolls itself into a ball and drops to the ground. When it lands it disappears into the undergrowth at great speed.

Vivarium: Type IV. This gecko prefers dense, finger-thick climbing branches.

Husbandry and reproduction: Several pairs may be kept together. Even the males are not aggressive towards one another. The females hide their 7 mm, almost spherical eggs beneath leaf mould. Incubation as for *U. ebenaui*. The young hatch after around 60 days measuring some 45 mm.

Uroplatus henkeli.

Uroplatus henkeli (Böhme & Ibisch, 1990)

Distribution: Madagascar and the island of Nosy Bé.

Habitat: To be found on tree trunks during the day. At night they spring from trunk to trunk or climb lianas to reach another tree. In this way they avoid going to ground level and falling prey to other animals. They only very rarely go to the upper reaches of the trees.

Size: 260 mm.

Left: Uroplatus sikorae sameiti.
Right: Uroplatus fimbriatus.

Characteristics: There is a considerable difference in colour between the sexes. The males have a yellow ground colour with several dark brown spots and stripes. The females are very finely spotted and the ground colour is usually beige-grey. In both sexes there is a fold of skin along each side of the entire body and along each side of the extremities. Whilst resting, this fold of skin blends in with the background so that no shadows are formed. The flat, serrated tail is laid over the backward-pointing legs. The camouflage is almost perfect. The entire appearance is that of a very flat creature.

Vivarium: Type IV. This species requires densely arranged, stout climbing branches. The height of the vivarium must not be less than 1 metre. Frequent spraying is essential.

Husbandry and reproduction: Several pairs may be kept in a large vivarium. When these animals concentrate on something, such as food or courtship, the tail is waved horizontally. In this way their excitement can be plainly seen. During mating the male does not employ a copulation bite. The female buries her eggs in the ground, and until they harden they are held by the hind feet. The eggs should be incubated in moist vermiculite. At 25 °C the young take over 90 days to hatch and measure around 60 mm. The eggs must not dry out during incubation. Although they are hard-shelled they require high atmospheric humidity. The young should be fed on small waxmoth larvae, small field crickets, and small house crickets. Adults eat all kinds of insects, including locusts and beetles.

Food: Locusts, beetles, crickets, waxmoth larvae, pink mice.

Similar species: *U. fimbriatus* and *U. sikorae sameiti* may be kept under the same conditions. The temperature range should be 18–30 °C. The species *U. sikorae sikorae* requires a constant atmospheric humidity of over 75% at temperatures of 15 °C at night and around 25 °C during the day. In their natural habitat during July and August, temperatures below 10 °C are not uncommon.

SUBFAMILY SPHAERODACTYLINAE
(BALL-FINGERED GECKOES)

Genus	Species	Distribution	Vivarium	Habitat
Coleodactylus	4	4	IV	A
Gonatodes	17	4, 4a, 4b, 5	III, IV	A
Lepidoblepharis	7	4, 4a	III, IV	A
Pseudogonatodes	4	4, 4a	III, IV	A
Sphaerodactylus	61	4, 4a, 4b, 5	III, IV	A

The subfamily of Sphaerodactylinae is found exclusively in the New World and is characterised by its undivided, ball-like clinging lamellae on the fingers. They are small geckoes, rarely reaching a length of 100 mm. All genera are distinguished by the fact that the female always lays only one egg.

Gonatodes (Fitzinger, 1843)

These are diurnal animals which occur in northern South America, in the Antilles, in Central America, and in Florida. Most species live on tree trunks. However, as followers of civilisation, they can also be found on house walls. All species show prominent sexual dimorphism. Whilst the males are conspicuously coloured, the females are mostly a grey colour. The females of all species lay only one hard-shelled egg. However, *G. humeralis* can lay up to twelve eggs in one year.

Gonatodes albogularis fuscus (Hallowell, 1855)

Distribution: Northern South America, Cuba, Central America.
Habitat: As followers of civilisation, this species can frequently be found amongst human habitation. In Cuba, this species lives on house walls in the centre of Havana.
Size: 100 mm.
Characteristics: The males are dark-grey, almost black and have a yellow head and a white tail-tip. The females are beige-brown with dark brown spots on the upper body. The narrow toes have a strong, nonretractile claw. This species has a round pupil, an indication of its diurnal lifestyle.
Vivarium: Type III. An attempt should be made to achieve an atmospheric humidity of around 75% at night. This can be done by spraying the vivarium each evening. During the day the temperature should be 25–28 °C. These animals pose no great demands on their surroundings. A vivarium of 40 × 30 × 30 cm is quite adequate for a pair. Several pieces of cork tube will frequently be used as hiding places.
Husbandry and reproduction: This species should be kept in pairs because even the females can be aggressive towards one another. It is impossible to keep two males together. The yellow head and white tail-tip work as signals, not only to animals of the same sex. During the year the female may lay up to nine individual eggs, usually left lying in the open. At a temperature of 28 °C the 38 mm young hatch after 55–65 days. Until shortly before sexual maturity, the young are the same colour as the females. This is also certainly the reason why the young are tolerated so long by the adults.
Food: Fruitfly, waxmoth larvae, small field crickets, small house crickets, house flies, and other small insects.

Gonatodes vittatus (Lichtenstein, 1856)

Distribution: Northern South America, Trinidad.
Habitat: The habitats are very divergent. This species lives on tree trunks, on cliffs, on walls, and is often found amongst piles of rocks on the ground. In general this species is regarded as a follower of civilisation.
Size: 85 mm.

Gonatodes fuscus.

Characteristics: *Gonatodes vittatus* is a very attractively coloured gecko which exhibits pronounced and colourful sexual dimorphism. The most significant characteristic of the males is the wide, white central stripe which runs from the tip of the snout to the tip of the tail, losing some of its intense colouring on the tail. The colouring of the body up to the black outline of the stripe is ochre and only the flanks and tail are grey. The females have a camouflage pattern composed of spots of various sizes and shapes. Newly hatched young have a similar colour and pattern. The scales are very small and fine.

Vivarium: Type III. The substrate should be a layer of forest loam upon which several flat rocks and pieces of cork bark are placed. Several pieces of cork bark or tree bark should be affixed to the rear and side walls. Thick branches and climbing plants complete the furnishings.

Husbandry and reproduction: This is a very lively and aggressive species which can only be kept in pairs. During the breeding period, from

Gonatodes vittatus.

April to September, the female may lay up to eight individual hard-shelled eggs which should be incubated at 25–28 °C and a relative atmospheric humidity of 60–80%. Under these conditions the young should hatch after 65–80 days. Juveniles should be reared individually in very small vivaria.

Food: Small field crickets, small house crickets, small and large wingless fruitfly, caterpillars, waxmoths, and mealworms.

Sphaerodactylus (Wagler, 1830)

These are the dwarfs amongst the geckoes. For example, *S. darlingtoni* only reaches a length of 40 mm. In comparison however, with a length of 70 mm, *S. cinereus* is the giant of this genus. The main distribution range of this genus is the entire Antilles Archipelago as well as Central America and northern South America. This species has probably also been introduced to the southern United States. Several species have adapted to changing habitats and can be found on house walls living as followers of civilisation. They are mainly crepuscular geckoes which are usually active in the early morning and early evening. The almost spherical pupil indicates that they are more diurnal than nocturnal. Some species exhibit significant sexual dimorphism. These creatures are predominantly ground dwellers living below leaf mould, wood, and rocks. They can climb extremely well using their nonretractile claws.

Sphaerodactylus darlingtoni (Shreve, 1968)

Distribution: Hispaniola, Dominican Republic.
Habitat: Moist forest regions with deep layers of leaf mould. They live on the ground, beneath leaf mould, and below rocks and wood. High humidity is essential.
Size: 40 mm.
Characteristics: The ground colour is brown with fine, dark-brown to black spots and stripes. On the head and in the neck area there are several light, half-moon-shaped stripes. At the front of the neck, between the forelegs, there are two white spots often edged in a darker colour.
Vivarium: Type III. A floor area of 30 × 30 cm is quite adequate for up to four animals. The height of the vivarium is of no importance since these animals live mainly at ground level. As hiding places, leaf mould and several pieces of cork bark should be placed on the bottom of the vivarium. High humidity is essential. Potting compost is a suitable substrate.
Husbandry and reproduction: With sufficient hiding places, two pairs can be kept under the conditions and dimensions mentioned above. The temperature range should be 20–25 °C with atmospheric humidity of 75%. The females hide the 6 × 4 mm egg on the ground beneath the leaf mould or below a piece of wood. Although the 10 mm young will not be attacked by the adults it is better to rear them separately so that their progress may be more easily checked. The young are identical to the parents.
Food: Small wingless fruitfly, springtails, greenfly (unsprayed), and small ermine moths.

Sphaerodactylus difficilis (Barbour, 1914)

Distribution: Hispaniola, Dominican Republic.

Habitat: This species may be regarded as a follower of civilisation and as such may be found on the wells of houses and in hotel complexes. These animals frequently climb.

Size: 50 mm.

Characteristics: The ground colour may be grey to brown. Over the entire upper body there are dark brown spots which sometimes join together to give a striped pattern. In some populations the males have a yellow head.

Vivarium: Type III. The vivarium for this species must be at least 40 cm high. A small dry-stone wall will frequently be used for climbing. The humidity should be as high as for the previous species.

Husbandry and reproduction: Several females may be kept with one male. Every 4–6 weeks the females will lay a single egg measuring 8 × 6 mm. Up to six eggs may be laid each year. The eggs are hidden beneath the leaf mould. In the wild the eggs are frequently found in termite mounds. Eggs should be incubated in a ventilated transparent container on a slightly moist substrate. Ventilation is essential because without it and with 100% humidity the eggs would quickly become mouldy. The eggs are best incubated at around 28 °C. On hatching, the young measure around 30 mm, and it is only wise to rear them with the adult animals when sufficient minute food is available for them. The young of this species grow very quickly.

Food: Fruitfly, springtails, minute waxmoth larvae, the larvae of the small ermine moth, and any other very small insects.

Bibliography

Abraham, G. (1983): Pflege und Zucht von verschiedenen Bodengeckoarten unter gleichen Haltungsbedingunggen. Sauria, 5: 5–11.

— (1985): *Teratoscincus scincus*. Beilage in Sauria, Amph.-/Rept.-Kartei: 27–28.

Angel, F. (1942): Les Lézards de Madagascar. Memoires de L'academie, Malgache XXXVI.

Arnold, E. N. (1980): A Review of the Lezard Genus *Stenodactylus*. Fauna Saudi Arabia, Riejadh, 2: 368–404.

Bartmann, W. und Minuth, E. (1979): Ein lebendgebärender Gecko *Rhacodactylus trachyrhynchus* Bocae 1973, aus Neukaledonien (Reptilia: Sauria: Gekkonidae). Salamandra 15, 1: 58–60.

Bauer, A. M. (1985): Notes on the taxonomy, morphology and behavior of *Rhacodactylus chahoua* (Bavay) (Reptilia: Gekkonidae). Bonn. zool. Beitr. 36: 81–94.

Bauer, A. M. und Russell, A. P. (1986): *Hoplodactylus delcourti* n. sp. (Reptilia: Gekkonidae), the largest known gecko. New Zealand Journal of Zoology, Vol. 13: 141–148.

— (1987): *Hoplodactylus delcourti* (Reptilia: Gekkonidae) and the Kawekaweau of Maori Folklore. J. Ethnobiol. 7: 83–91.

— (1989): A Systematic Review of The Genus *Uroplatus* (Reptilia: Gekkonidae), with Comments on its Biology. Universität Calgary.

Bellairs, A. (1948): The eyelids and spectacle in geckos. Proc. Zool. Soc. London, 118: 420–425.

— (1969): Die Reptilien. Weidenfeld und Nicholson, London.

Blüm, V. (1985): Vergleichende Reproduktionsbiologie der Wirbeltiere. Springer Verlag, Berlin/Heidelberg/New York/Tokyo.

BNA (1987): Das neue Artenschutzrecht. BNA-Handbuch, Köln.

Böhme, W. und Meier, H. (1980): Revision der madagassischen *Homopholis* (*Blaesodactylus*)-Arten (Sauria: Gekkonidae). Senck. biol. 60: 303–315.

Böhme, W. (1981): Handbuch der Reptilien und Amphibien Europas, Band I. Akademische Verlagsgesellschaft, Wiesbaden.

— (1981): Eine neue Form der *madagascariensis*-Gruppe der Gattung *Phelsuma* von den Seychellen (Reptilia: Sauria: Gekkonidae). Salamandra 17: 12–19.

— (1984): Erstfund eines fossilen Kugelfingergeckos (Sauria: Gekkonidae: Sphaero-
    dactylinae) aus dem Dominikanischen Bernstein. Salamandra 20, 4: 212–220.
— (1985): Zur Nomenklatur der paläarktischen Bodenfingergeckos, Gattung *Tenui-
    dactylus* Scerbak & Golubew, 1984. Bonn. zool. Beitr., 36, 1/2: 95–98.
— und Henkel, F. W. (1985): Zur Kenntnis der Herpetofauna Neukaledoniens, speziell
    der Gattung *Rhacodactylus*. herpetofauna 7, 34: 23–29.
— und Ibisch, P. (1990): Studien an *Uroplatus*. I. Der *Uroplatus-fimbriatus-* Komplex.
    Salamandra 26, 4: 246–259.
Bourne, A. R., Taylor, J. L. und Watson, T. G. (1986): Annual cycles of plasma and tes-
    ticular androgens in the lizard *Tiliqua rugosa*. Gen. comp. Endocr. 61: 278–286.
Branch, B. (1988): Field Guide to the Snakes and other Reptiles of Southern Africa.
    New Holland, London.
Broer, W. (1978): Rotschwanznatter *Goniosoma oxycephala*, ihre Pflege und Zucht. Das
    Aquarium 12: 79–81.
Bull, J. J. (1980): Sex determination in reptiles. The Quarterly Review of Biology. 55, 1:
    3–21.
Bustard, H. R. (1966): The *Oedura tryoni* complex: East Australian Rock-Dwelling
    Geckos (Reptilia: Gekkonidae). Bulletin of the British Museum Zoology, Lon-
    don, 14, 1: 1–14.
— (1970): *Oedura marmorata a complex of Australian geckos (Reptilia: Gekkonidae).*
    Senck. biol. 51: 21–40.
Cogger, H. G. (1988): Reptiles & Amphibians of Australia. Reed, Sydney.
Cooper, J. E. und Jackson, O. F., eds. (1981): Diseases of the Reptilia. Vol. 1 & 2, Aca-
    demic Press, London/New York/Toronto/Sydney/San Francisco.
Duvall, R. A., Guilette, L. J. und Jones, R. E. (1982): Environmental control of reptilian
    reproductive cycles. In: Gans, C. (Hrsg.), Biology of reptilia.
Eijsden, E. H. T. v. (1983): Der haftfähige Greifschwanz des Europäischen Blattfinger-
    geckos *Phyllodactylus europaeus*. Salamandra 19, 1/2: 1–10.
Fitzsimons, V. F. (1943): The Lizards of South Africa, Trans. Mus. Men. 1, XV: 1–528.
Fox, H. (1977): The urogential system of reptiles. In: Gans, C. (Hrsg.), Biology of rep-
    tiles.
Frankenberg, E. (1978): Calls of male and female tree geckos, *Cyrtodactylus kotschyi*.
    Israel J. Zool. 27: 53–56.
Friederich, U. and Volland, W. (1981): Futtertierzuchten. Verlag Eugen Ulmer,
    Stuttgart.
Frolow, W. E. (1981): Fortpflanzung des Wundergeckos, *Teratoscincus scincus* im
    Moskauer Zool. Garten. Jena 51, 3/4: 263–266.
Gans, C. (ab 1969): Biology of the reptilia. Academic Press, New York, Vol. 1–15.
Grismer, L. L. (1988): Phylogeny, taxonomy, classification and biogeography of euble-
    pharid geckos. In: Estes, R. & Pregili, G. (Hrsg.), Phytogenetic relationships of the
    lizard families. Stanford/Calif., 369–469.
Haacke, W. D. (1976): The Burrowing Geckos of Southern Africa. Ann. Transv. Mus. 30:
    53–70.

Hagedorn, H. (1973): Beobachtungen zum Verhalten von Phelsumen im Terrarium. Salamandra 9, 2/3: 137–144.

Hallmann, G. (1984): Verzeichnis von 180 Publikationen über die Gekkonidengattung *Phelsuma*. Selbstverlag, Dortmund.

Heimes, P. (1987): Beitrag zur Systematik der Fächerfinger. Salamandra, Frankfurt, 23, 4: 212–235.

Henkel, F. W (1981): Pflege und Nachzucht von *Rhacodactylus chahoua*. DATZ 34, 2: 68–70.

— (1986a): Bemerkungen über einige *Rhacodactylus*-Arten. herpetofauna, 8, 42: 6–8.

— (1986b): *Rhacodactylus chachoua*. Beilage in Sauria, Amph.-/Rept.-Kartei 51–52.

— (1987): Pflege und Zucht von *Chrondrodactylus angulifer*. DATZ 5: 227–229.

— (1988): *Rhacodactylus sarasinorum*. Beilage in Sauria, Amph.-/Rept.-Kartei 125–128.

— (1989a): Erfahrungen mit dem Grünen Baumgecko. DATZ 4: 212–213.

— (1989b): Erfahrungen mit dem Gecko *Hoplodactylus granulatus*. DATZ 8: 468–470.

Henkel, F. W. und Zobel, R. (1987): Zur Kenntnis des Bronzegeckos, *Ailuronyx seychellensis*. Herpetofauna 9: 12–14.

Heselhaus, R. (1986): Taggeckos. Verlag Reimar Hobbing GmbH, Essen.

Hiller, U. (1968): Untersuchungen zum Feinbau und zur Funktion der Haftborsten von Reptilien. Z. Moroph. Tiere, 62: 307–362.

Hoesch, U. (1981): Nachzuchten. Sauria, 3: 26–27.

Ippen, R., Schröder, H.-D. und Elze, K. (1985): Handbuch der Zootierkrankheiten, Band 1: Reptilien. Akademie-Verlag, Berlin.

Isenbügel, E. und Frank, W. (1985): Heimtierkrankheiten. Verlag Eugen Ulmer, Stuttgart.

Jes, H. (1987): Echsen als Terrarientiere. Gräfe und Unzer GmbH, München.

Joger, U. (1984): Morphologische und biochemische-immunologische Untersuchungen der Gattung *Tarentola*. Zool. Jb. Anat. 112: 137–256.

Kästle, W. (1964): Verhaltensstudien an Taggeckonen der Gattungen *Lygodactylus* und *Phelsuma*. Z. f. Tierpsycholo. 21, 4: 486–507.

— (1974): Echsen im Terrarium. Franckh'sche Verlagshandlung, Stuttgart.

King, M. (1977): The evolution of sex chromosomes in lizard. In: Calaby, J. & Tyndale-Briscoe, H. (Hrsg.), Evolution and reproduction. Australien Academy of Science, Canberra, 55–60.

Klejch, W. (1974): Der indische Hausgecko (*Hemidactylus flaviviridis*). DATZ, 27: 175–177.

Klingelhöffer, W. (1957): Terrarienkunde, 3. Teil. Kernen, Stuttgart.

Kluge, A. G. (1967): Higher Taxonomic Categories of Gekkonid Lizards and Their Evolution. Bull. Am. Nat. Hist. 135: 1–59.

— (1987): C'ladistic relationships in the Gekkonidae (Squamata, Sauria). Misc. Publ. Mus. Zool. Univ. Michigan 173: 1–54.

Knötig, M. (in Vorbereitung): Überarbeitung der Liste der rezenten Gekkonidae.

Krintler, K. (1982): Die Geckos der Gattung *Gonatodes* auf Trinidad und Tobago. DATZ 35: 349–350.

Licht, P., Hoyer, H. E. und van Oordt, P. G.: W. J. (1969): Influence of photoperiod and temperature on testicular recrudescence and body growth in the lizards. J. Zoology, London, 157: 469-501.

Lilge, D. und van Meeuwen, H. (1979): Grundlagen der Terrarienhaltung. Landbuch-Verlag GmbH, Hannover.

— overidge, A. (1947): Revision of the African Lizards of the Family Gekkonidae. Bull. Mus. Comp. Zool. 98, 1: 1-469.

Manthey, U. (1982): Die Gattung *Ptychozoon* Kuhl, 1822 (Faltengeckos), mit einem Bestimmungsschlüssel für die fünf Arten. Teil 1 und 2. Sauria 4: 11-17.

Maronde, M. (1986): *Cyrtodactylus pulchellus*. Beilage in Sauria, Amph.-/Rept.-Kartei: 63-64.

Mau, K.-G. (1978): Nachweis natürlicher Parthenogenese bei *Lepidodactylus lugubris* durch Gefangenschaftsnachzucht. Salamandra 14, 2: 90-97.

Meier, H. (1975): Phelsumen, auf Madagaskar beobachtet. Aquarium mit Aquaterra 9: 169-173, 218-222.

— (1977): Beobachtungen an *Phelsuma standingi* (Reptilia, Sauria, Gekkonidae). Salamandra 13: 1-12.

— (1979): Herpetologische Beobachtungen auf Neukaledonien. Salamandra 15, 3: 113-119.

— (1980): Zur Lebendfärbung, Lebensweise und zum Verbreitungsgebiet von *Phelsuma guttata* Kaudern, 1922 (Reptilia, Sauria, Gekkonidae). Salamandra 16: 2-88.

— (1981): Zur Taxonomie und Ökologie der Gattung *Phelsuma* auf den Komoren, mit Beschreibung einer neuen Art. Bonn, zool. Beitr. 31: 323-332.

— (1987): Vorläufige Beschreibung einer neuen Art der Gattung *Phelsuma* von Madagaskar. Salamandra 23, 4: 204-211.

— (1989): Zur Faunistik madagassischer Taggeckos der Gattung *Phelsuma* östlich von Fianarantsoa, bei Tamatave und auf der Insel St. Marie. Salamandra 25: 224-229.

— (1989): Eine neue Form aus der *lineata*-Gruppe der Gattung *Phelsuma* auf Madagaskai. Salamandra 25: 230-236.

Mertens, R. (1946): Die Warn- und Drohreaktion der Reptilien. Abh. senck. nat. Ges. 471: 1-108.

— (1954): Studien über die Reptilienfauna Madagaskars II. Senck. biol. 35: 13-16.

— (1955): Über eine eigenartige Rasse des Tokees aus Ost-Pakistan. Senck. biol. 36: 21-24.

— (1958): Neue Eidechsen aus Australien. Senck. biol. 39: 51-56.

— (1962): Studien über die Reptilienfauna Madagaskars III. Senck. biol. 43: 81-126.

— (1963): Studien über die Reptilienfauna Madagaskars IV. Senck. biol. 44: 349-356.

— (1964): Neukaledonische Riesengeckos (*Rhacodactylus*). Zool. Garten, Leipzig, N. F. 29: 49-57.

— (1966): Die nichtmadagassischen Arten und Unterarten der Geckonengattung *Phelsuma*. Senck. biol. 47: 85-100.

— (1970): Neues über einige Taxa der Geckonengattung *Phelsuma*. Senck. biol. 51: 1-13.

— (1973): Eine neue Unterart der Taggeckos *Phelsuma lineata*. Senck. biol. 54: 199–301.

— (1973): Der typische Fundort von *Phelsuma dubia* (Sauria, Gekkonidae). Salamandra 9: 75–77.

Mitchell, F. J. (1965): Australian geckos assigned to the genus *Gehyra*. Senck. biol. 46: 287–319.

Mudrack, W. (1976): Der fliegende Gecko—ein Meister der Tarnung. Aquarien Magazin 160–163.

— (1985): *Teratoscincus microlepis*. Beilage in Sauria, Amph.-/Rept.-Kartei: 9–10.

Müller, M. J. (1983): Handbuch ausgewählter Klimastationen der Erde, Trier.

Nettmann, H. K. und Rykena, S. (1979): Mauergeckos, die ihre Eier im Sand vergraben. Salamandra 15, 1: 53–57.

Nietzke, G. (1978): Die Terrarientiere 1 und 2. Verlag Eugen Ulmer, Stuttgart.

— (1990): Zur Durchlässigkeit von UV-Strahlen der Reptilienhaut. Salamandra 26, 1: 50–57.

Obst, F. J., Richter, K., Jacob, U. et al. (1984): Lexikon der Terraristik und Herpetologie. Landbuchverlag, Hannover.

Osadnik, G. (1987): Untersuchungen zur Reproduktionsbiologie des madagassischen Taggeckos *Phelsuma dubia* (Boettger, 1881). Dissertation Universität Bochum.

Petzold, H. G. (1982): Aufgaben und Probleme bei der Erforschung der Lebensäußerungen der Niederen Ammionten (Reptilean). Berliner Tierpark, Buch Nr. 38. Nachdruck aus Milu Bd. 5 (4/5): 485–786.

Philippen, H. D. (1989): Neue Erkenntnisse bei der temperaturabhängigen Geschlechtsfixierung. herpetofauna 11, 61: 22–24.

— (1990): Checkliste der rezenten Taggeckos (*Phelsuma*). Unveröffentlicht.

Podloucky, R. (1987): Das neue Artenschutzrecht und seine Folgen für die Amphibien- und Reptilienhaltung. herpetofauna 9 (50): 9–16.

Ravet, J. (1948): Atlas climatographique de Madagascar. Publ. Serv. meteorolique Madagascar, Antananarivo, 10: 1–96.

Remy, A. und Remy, A. (1990): Zur Haltung und Zucht von *Stenodactylus sthenodactylusz*. Herpetofauna 12: 6–9.

Rieppel, O. (1973): Zur Kenntnis von *Gekkonia chazaliae*. Aquarien Terrarien 7: 230–233.

Robb, J. (1980): New Zealand Amphibians & Reptiles. Williams Collins Pub. Ltd., Auckland.

Rösler, H. (1980a): Fang, Haltung und Eiablage des Kammzehengeckos *Crossobamon sobamon eversmanni*. Elaphe 3: 33–35.

— (1980b): Geschlechtsbestimmung bei Gekkoniden anhand von Hautreservaten. Salamandra 16, 4: 266–268.

— (1981a): Ohne Besonderheiten?-*Gekko monarchus* (D. & B., 1836). Sauria 3: 7–11.

— (1981b): Erfolg und Mißerfolg bei der Vermehrung von *Hemitheconyx caudicinctus* in Gefangenschaft. Elaphe 4: 49–54.

— (1982a): Etwas über das Alter von Gekkonen. Elaphe 3: 40–41.

— (1982b): Ein terraristisches Kleinod: Der Sandgecko. Aquarien Magazin 10: 587-588.

— (1983): Vergleichende Studien zum Warn- und Drohverhalten bodenbewohnender Geckonen. Salamandra 19, 4: 211-227.

— (1988): Über das »Eierfressen« im Terrarium bei Arten der Gattung *Phelsuma*. Salamandra 24, 1: 20-26.

— (1990): Kaokogecko *vanzyli*, ein seltener Terrarienbewohner. DATZ 5: 273-274.

Roux, J. (1913): Les Reptiles de la Nouvelle-Caledonie et des iles Loyalty. Nova Caledonia, A. Zoologie I, Wiesbaden: 79-160.

Russell, A. P. (1972): The foot of gekkonid lizards: A study in comparative and functional anatomy. Unpublished Ph.D. thesis, University of London.

— (1977): Comments concerning post-cloacal bones in geckos (Reptilia: Gekkonidae). Canad. J. Zool. 55, 7: 1201-1205.

Sameit, J. (1986): *Rhacodactylus auriculatus*. Beilage in Sauria, Amph.-/Rept.-Kartei 8, 2: 43-44.

— (1988): *Rhacodactylus trachyrhynchus*. Beilage in Sauria, Amph.-/Rept.-Kartei 10, 1: 99-100.

— (1988): Asper & Co., Australische Knopfschwanzgeckos. DATZ 6: 162-164.

Scerbak, N. N. und Golubev, M. L. (1986): Gekkonii faunii CCCP i ssopredjedjel'nych sstran. Kiew. (In Russian).

Schröder, E. (1987): Beobachtungen an 16 Nachzuchtgenerationen des madagassichen Geckos *Paroedura pictus*. Salamandra 23, 4: 236-240.

Schubert, Ch. und Christophers, E. (1984): Dermolytische Schreckhäutung—ein besonderes Autotomieverhalten von *Geckolepis typica* (Reptilia, Gekkonidae). Zoologischer Anzeiger Jena 214 (3/4): 129-141.

Schwartz, A. und Thomas, R. (1983): The Difficilis Complex of *Sphaerodactylus* (Sauria, Gekkonidae) of Hispanola. Bulletin of Carnegie Museum of Natural History, Pittsburgh.

Seipp, R. (1991): Eine neue Art der Gattung *Phelsuma*, Gray 1825, von Madagaskar. Senck. biol. 71, 1/3, 11-14.

Seufer, H. (1979a): Haltung und Nachzucht von Kaspischen Nacktfinger-Geckos. DATZ 32: 61-63.

— (1979b): Der Kaspische Geradfinger-Gecko (*Alsophylax pipiens*), Pallas. herpetofauna 1, 1: 10-15.

— (1985): Geckos. APV, Minden.

— (1988): Haltung und Zucht des Helmkopfgeckos *Geckonia chazaliae* Mocquard, 1895 in zweiter Generation. Sauria 10, 2: 21-25.

Simkiss, K. (1967): Calcium in reproductive physiology. Chapman and Hall, London.

Stettler, P. H. (1987): Handbuch der Terrarienkunde. Franckh'sche Verlagshandlung, Stuttgart.

Taylor, E. H. (1963): The Lizards of Thailand. Univ. Kansas Sci. Bull. Vol. 44, 14: 687-1077.

Ulber, Th. (1989): Zur Verbreitung und Merkmalsvariabilität von *Cyrtodactylus peguensis*. Sauria 11: 3-9.

Ulber, Th. und E. (1987a): Auf der Mauer, auf der Lauer—Erfahrungen mit der Zimmerhaltung von verschiedenen Geckos. Sauria 9, 2: 7-12.

— (1987b): *Pachydactylus bibronii*. Beilage in Sauria, Amph.-/Rept.-Kartei: 81-86.

Ulber, Th. und Gericke, F. (1988): Zur Problematik der Verwandtschaftsverhältnisse in der Gattung *Cyrtodactylus* Gray, 1827 und Bemerkungen zur Gattung *Nactus* Kluge, 1983 (Reptilia: Sauria: Gekkonidae). Der Versuch einer—auch philosophischen—Analyse. Veröff. Naturhist. Mus. Schleusingen 3: 67-74.

Ulber, Th. und Grossmann, W. (1991): Ein weiterer neuer Gecko aus Zentral-Thailand: *Cyrtodactylus papilionoides* sp. nov. Sauria 13, 1: 13-22.

Ulber, Th., Grossmann, W., Beutelschiess, J. und Beutelschiess, Ch. (1989): Terraristisch/Herpetologisches Fachwörterbuch. Terrariengemeinschaft Berlin e. V., Berlin.

Ulber, Th. und Schäfer, Ch. (1989): *Cyrtodactylus peguensis*. Beilage in Sauria, Amph.-/Rept.-Kartei 145-148.

Underwood, G. (1954): On the Classification and Evolution of Geckos. Proc. zool. Soc. London 124: 469-492.

Wermuth, H. (1965): Liste der rezenten Amphibien und Reptilien: Gekkonidae, Pygopodidae, Xantusiidae. In: Das Tierreich. Berlin, Lfg. 80: 1-246.

Werner, Y. L. (1966): Über die israelischen Geckos der Gattung *Ptyodactylus* und ihre Biologie. Salamandra 1: 15-25.

— (1967): Regeneration of the Caudal Axial Skeleton in a Gekkonid Lizard (*Hemidactylus*) with Particular Reference to the »Latent« Period. Acta Zoologica, Bd. XLVII: 103-125.

Wilson, S. K. und Knowles, D. G. (1988): Australia's Reptiles. William Collins Pty. Ltd., Sydney.

Zielger, H. & W. (1989): *Palmatogecko rangei*. Beilage in Sauria, Amph.-/Rept.-Kartei 129-132.

Zimmerman, E. (1983): Das Züchten von Terrarientieren. Franckh'sche Verlagshandlung, Stuttgart.

Illustrations

The line drawings were prepared by Marianne Lippe, Dortmund.

Photographs by:

Michael Knötig, Borken, 165
Klaus Liebel, Herne, ii, 80, 103, 171, 179, 182, 190 right, 199.
Joachim Sameit, Bergkamen, 110, 123, 124, 157, 190 left, 217 left and right.
Rainer Stockey, Hohenlimburg, 9.
Thomas Ulber, Berlin, 145, 154.

All other photographs by the authors.

Index